To my wonderful grandma, may you always know that you were the reason I fell in love with crocheting. This book is all because of you.

To my husband, Carl. Thank you for always loving and supporting me, even though I may be crazy sometimes!

To my mom, thank you for telling me I could do it even when I wanted to give up. I love you!

paige tate & co.

Copyright © 2018 Lauren Espy
Published by Blue Star Press
Paige Tate & Co. is an imprint of Blue Star Press
PO Box 8835, Bend, OR 97708
contact@paigetate.com | www.paigetate.com

Photography and instructions by Lauren Espy
@amenagerieofstitches
Etsy® Shop: A Menagerie of Stitches

ISBN 9781944515638

Printed in China

11 10 9 8 7 6 5 4 3

Modern Makers Series

PAIGE TATE & CO.

WHIMSICAL STITCHES

a Modern Makers Book of Amigurumi Crochet Patterns

LAUREN ESPY

TABLE OF CONTENTS

4

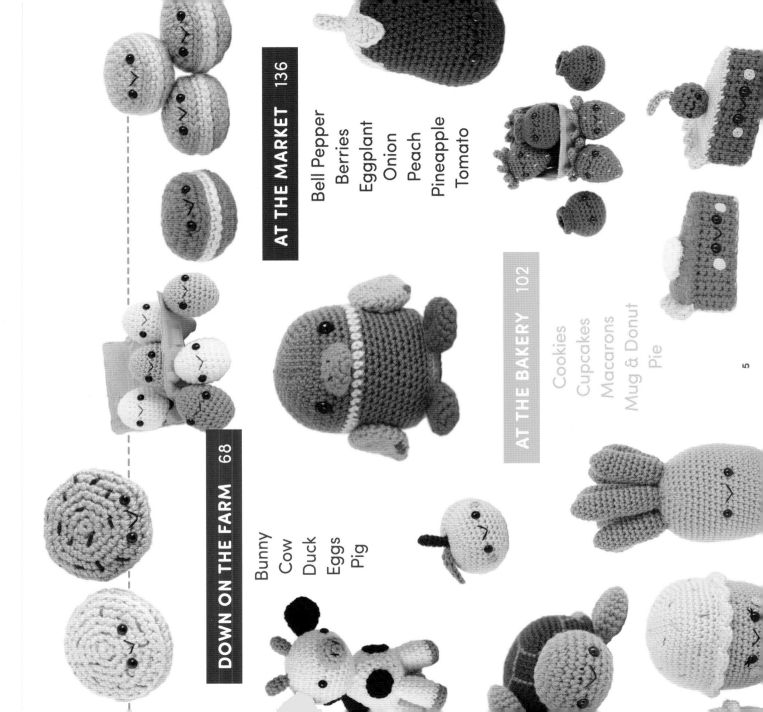

Hello, and welcome! My name is Lauren and I'm so glad you are here!

My crochet journey began in 2009 when my grandmother bought me a book about amigurumi. I was intrigued that something so cute and small could be made by using yarn and a hook. My grandma, being the wonderful person she was, purchased the book for me and later gifted me a full set of crochet hooks. I spent hours trying to teach myself to crochet, and there were many times when I felt like I would never figure it out. After countless tries and lots of YouTube® videos, something finally clicked. I was hooked!

When I first started crocheting, I used patterns from books or ones I found online. I knew I eventually wanted to design my own patterns, but I was so nervous to try. The great thing with amigurumi, though, is that once you have mastered a few basic shapes, you can crochet almost anything! I sat and sketched out little kawaii characters, and then I pulled out the yarn and dove in. Since then, I've been designing all my own patterns and sharing what I make with the world. Being able to crochet something that was just an idea on paper has to be my favorite part of knowing how to crochet.

In 2015 I finally opened my Etsy® shop, A Menagerie of Stitches. Many people know me as the girl who crocheted a chemistry set, but I promise I've crocheted much more than that! I love adding faces to inanimate objects, and my Instagram™ feed is always filled with smiling food, plants, and animals. The items I crochet are things that I love to keep around the house, and make me smile when I see them.

So go on and crochet! I hope you enjoy this book and have fun making all sorts of cute things to gift or keep for yourself. Whether you're a beginner or expert crocheter, I have a feeling you're going to love these patterns and the items you make.

Happy crocheting!

Lauren Espy

MATERIALS AND TOOLS

To complete the patterns in this book, here are some of the materials and tools you will need:

YARN:
You'll want to use worsted #4 weight yarn for all the projects in this book. Worsted weight comes in a large variety of colors and brands. Choose your favorite colors, or those recommended for each pattern.

CROCHET HOOKS:
Most of the patterns contained in this book use a U.S. size G-4.25mm crochet hook. Be aware that if you change the hook size, your items may come out a different size than what the pattern states.

SAFETY EYES:
Safety eyes come in all sorts of sizes and colors. They can range anywhere from 6mm to 40mm. Most of the patterns in this book require size 12mm, 9mm or 6mm. Safety eyes come with a plastic or metal washer that attaches to the back and makes the eye nearly impossible to remove. Make sure you've positioned the eyes exactly where you'd like them before attaching the backs. Buttons are a great alternative if you can't find safety eyes.

Note: if you plan on giving the items you create to small children, I always recommend replacing the safety eyes with felt or embroidering them on using yarn or thread.

STUFFING:
I always use polyester fiberfill to stuff my amigurumis. Make sure to add enough so your item won't lose shape, but take care not to add too much. Over-stuffing can cause the fabric to stretch and the stuffing to show through the stitches.

YARN NEEDLE:
Also called a darning needle, this needle is great because it has a bigger eye which makes threading yarn onto it much easier. This is an ideal needle to use to attach crocheted pieces together.

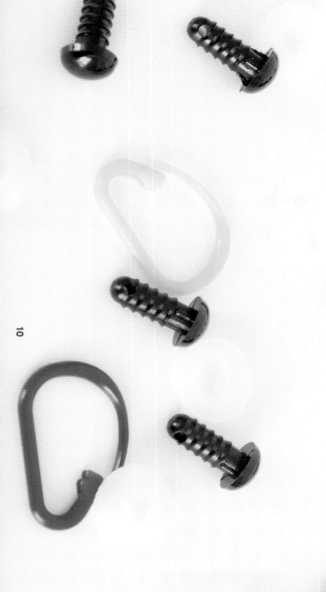

EMBROIDERY FLOSS AND NEEDLE:

You can use embroidery floss to add facial features. Floss comes in all sorts of colors, just like yarn. I always use black for the mouths and eyelashes. Embroidery floss can also be used to add smaller details, such as rosy cheeks.

FELT:

Felt is another great material to use for facial features like eyes or rosy cheeks.

STITCH MARKERS:

Stitch markers are your best friend when crocheting amigurumi! Amigurumi is crocheted "in the round" so use these to mark the start or end of each round. If you don't want to purchase markers, items you might have around the house (like safety pins) also work great!

SCISSORS:

Have a sharp pair of scissors on hand for trimming yarn or embroidery floss.

STRAIGHT PINS:

Straight pins are great to use as positioning aids before you sew the pieces on.

OTHER MATERIALS YOU MAY NEED

CARDBOARD: Cardboard can be useful for making the bases of items more sturdy.

PIPE CLEANERS: Pipe cleaners (also known as chenille stems) are perfect to use as flower stems.

POLY PELLETS AND SCRAP FABRIC: These items can be used to make a "bean bag" to help items stand up.

TERRA COTTA POTS: These pots are essential for planting the flowers you stitch!

WOODEN DOWELS: Dowels can be used for flower stems and support.

HOT GLUE GUN: Use a hot glue gun to assemble flowers to the pots.

EGG CARTON OR BERRY BOX: Use a cardboard egg carton or a cute berry box to display your creations!

ABBREVIATIONS

Approx – Approximately

Ch – Chain

Dc – Double crochet

Hdc – Half double crochet

Inv dec – Invisible decrease

Mr – Magic ring (also known as adjustable ring)

R – Round

Row

Sc – Single crochet

Sk – Skip

Sl St – Slip stitch

St(s) – Stitch(es)

Tr – Triple crochet

* – Repeat the directions in between * and * as many times as stated.

( ) – The number inside will indicate how many stitches you should have at the end of each round.

RESOURCES

Yarn, needles, and other supplies can be purchased from a wide variety of retailers. These are some of my go-to sources for materials!

Caron Yarn
www.yarnspirations.com/caron

Lion Brand Yarn
www.lionbrandyarn.com

Red Heart Yarn
www.redheart.com

Safety Eyes
Local craft stores might carry safety eyes, but if you are having difficulty finding them, try sites like www.etsy.com or www.freshstitches.com for a variety of safety eye options.

STITCHES AND TECHNIQUES

GAUGE:

The measurements provided for each item in this book are approximate. Depending on your tension, yarn, and hook size, your items may turn out a little bigger or smaller.

YARN OVER:

To yarn over, simply grab hold of the yarn with your hook. The yarn will be going over your hook and then you can proceed to pull it through the loops or stitch.

MAGIC RING (also known as an adjustable ring):

I prefer this method because it makes the piece close up more, and a small hole isn't left at the top.

TO MAKE A MAGIC RING:
(steps pictured on opposite page)

1. Make a loop and place the working yarn on top of the loose tail.
2. Insert hook into loop, grabbing the working yarn with the hook. Pull through the loop.
3. Yarn over and pull hook through loop.

This is where you will start making single crochets into the magic ring.

4. Insert the hook back into the loop; make sure to go underneath both yarn tails.
5. Yarn over and pull hook through loop. 2 loops will be on the hook.
6. Yarn over and pull through both loops. This completes your first single crochet.
7. Repeat as many times as pattern states.
8. Grab the loose tail and pull to close the loop.
9. Begin crocheting, starting in the first single crochet from step 6.

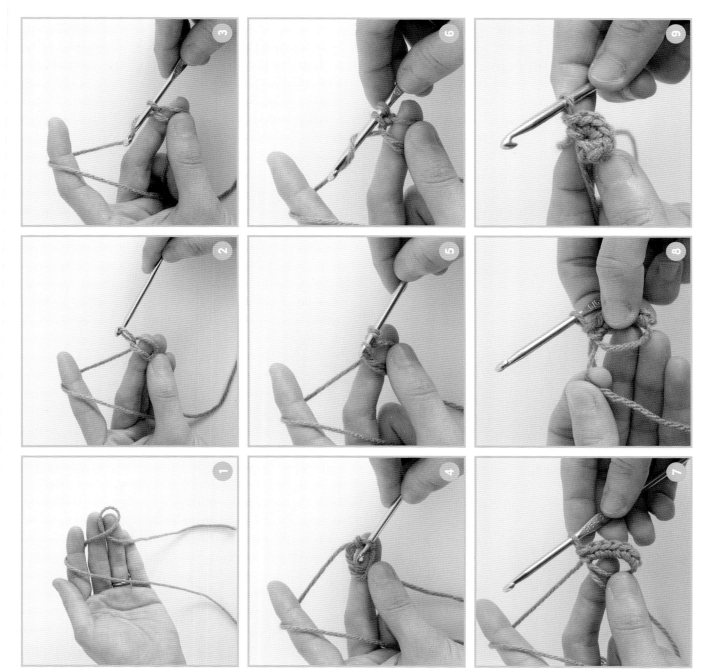

SINGLE CROCHET:

1. Insert hook into stitch and yarn over. Pull hook through stitch. There will be 2 loops on your hook (photos 1 & 2).
2. Yarn over again and pull through both loops. 1 loop will remain on hook (photos 3 & 4).

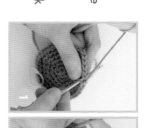

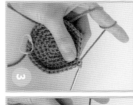

HALF DOUBLE CROCHET:

1. Yarn over and insert hook into stitch (photo 1).
2. Yarn over and pull hook through stitch; 3 loops will remain on hook (photos 2 & 3).
3. Yarn over and pull through all 3 loops. 1 loop will remain on hook (photos 4 & 5).

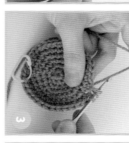
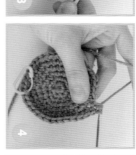
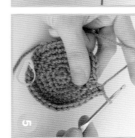

DOUBLE CROCHET:

1. Yarn over once and insert hook into stitch (photo 1).
2. Yarn over and pull hook through stitch; 3 loops will remain on hook (photo 2).
3. Yarn over and pull through 2 loops. 2 loops will remain on hook (photo 3).
4. Yarn over for a final time and pull hook through remaining 2 loops. 1 loop will remain on hook (photos 4 & 5).

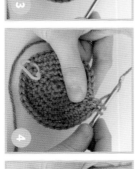
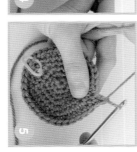

TRIPLE CROCHET:

1. Yarn over 2 times so that 3 loops are on hook *(photo 1)*.
2. Insert hook into stitch and yarn over *(photo 2)*. Pull hook through stitch. There will be 4 loops on your hook.
3. Yarn over and pull through 2 loops. 3 loops will remain on hook *(photos 3 & 4)*.
4. Yarn over again and pull through another 2 loops. 2 loops will remain on hook *(photos 5 & 6)*.
5. Yarn over for a final time and pull through the remaining 2 loops. 1 loop will remain on hook *(photo 7)*.

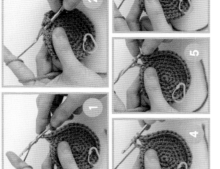

FRONT OR BACK LOOPS ONLY:

Some of the patterns in this book use this technique. In order to figure out which is the front and which is the back, simply hold your work up with the front of your work facing you. You will see a row of V's. The loops closest to you are the front loops *(photo 1)* and the farthest ones are the back loops *(photo 2)*.

INVISIBLE DECREASE:

1. Insert the hook into the FRONT loops only of the next 2 stitches. There will be 3 loops on your hook *(photo 1)*.
2. Yarn over and pull hook through 2 loops (the 2 front loops). 2 loops will remain on hook *(photos 2 & 3)*.
3. Yarn over again and pull through the 2 remaining loops. 1 loop will remain on hook *(photo 4)*.

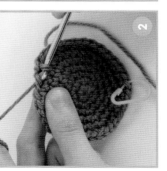

17

SLIP KNOT:

1. Make a loop and place the loose tail on top of the working yarn.

2. Insert hook into loop and grab the loose tail.

3. Pull the loose tail through the loop, but not all the way.

4. Pull the tail to tighten the slip knot onto the hook.

CHAIN:

1. After you have made a slip knot, simply take the the working yarn and yarn over.

2. Pull hook through the slip knot. This is your first chain stitch. Repeat as many times as the pattern states.

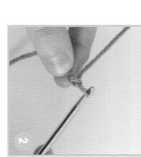

SLIP STITCH:

1. Insert hook into stitch or chain and yarn over.

2. Pull hook through stitch or chain. There will be 2 loops on your hook.

3. Pull hook through the first loop and 1 loop will remain on hook.

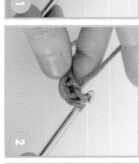

CLEAN COLOR CHANGING TECHNIQUE

1. When working the last stitch of the old color, do the typical single crochet until there are 2 loops left on the hook (photo 1).

2. Use the new color to yarn over and pull through those 2 loops (photo 2).

3. Sl St into the next stitch with the new color (photos 3 & 4).

4. Continue to crochet as normal with the new color (photo 5).

5. Trim the tail of the old color. Tie the tails from both colors together to secure the color change.

 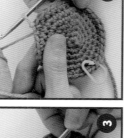 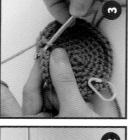 

CLOSING UP YOUR PIECE

I like to use the following closing technique because it give the piece a more finished look, and the closure is nearly invisible.

1. When you've reached the end of the piece, cut the yarn and leave a tail for sewing. Pull yarn tail through the loop on the hook and pull to secure (photo 1).

2. Thread the yarn tail onto the needle. Insert the needle into the front loop of the first stitch, working from the center to the outside. Pull needle through. Continue going through the front loops of the remaining stitches (photo 2).

3. Once you have reached the end, pull the yarn tail and the hole will close (photo 3).

4. Insert the needle into the center of the hole and bring out to the other side (where the magic ring is). Trim the yarn close to the piece and hide the tail inside (photos 4 & 5).

ADDING EYELASHES

Thread your sewing needle with a length of embroidery floss.

1. Bring the needle from inside the piece to the outside. Make sure your needle is right next to the safety eye (photo 1).

2. Insert the needle back into the piece, about ¼ of an inch away from the eye to make the first lash (photos 2 & 3).

3. Bring the needle to the outside again, and repeat step 2 for making another lash. Make sure to place the lashes apart from each other (photo 4).

4. Once the needle is inside the piece and you have sewn on as many lashes as you'd like, make a knot to secure floss.

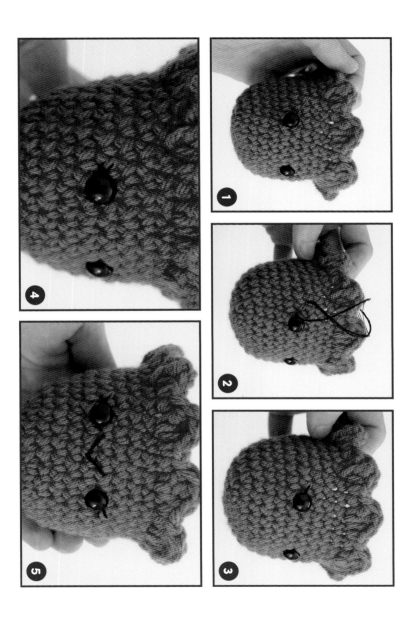

ADDING A MOUTH

Thread your sewing needle with a length of embroidery floss.

1. Bring the needle from inside the piece to the outside, near the safety eye on your left (*photo 1*).
2. Go across to the right side and insert needle into piece. Don't pull the needle all the way through (*photo 2*).
3. Hold the thread in a smile shape and bring the needle up into the center and down a stitch or two (*photo 3*).
4. Pull thread down to make a "V" shape (*photo 4*).
5. Insert the needle close to the spot where the needle first came out at to create the smile (*photo 5*).
6. Pull thread through and make a knot to secure floss (*photo 6*).

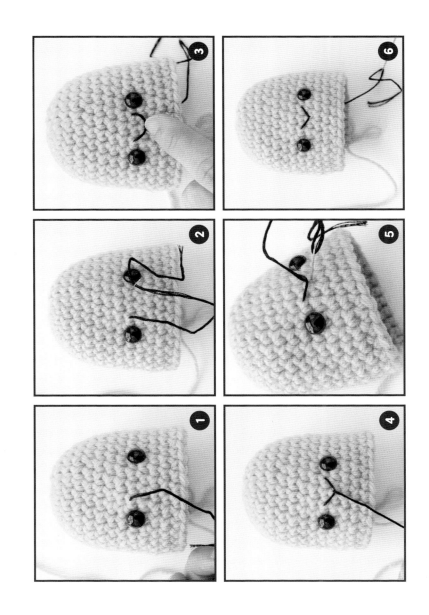

IN THE GARDEN

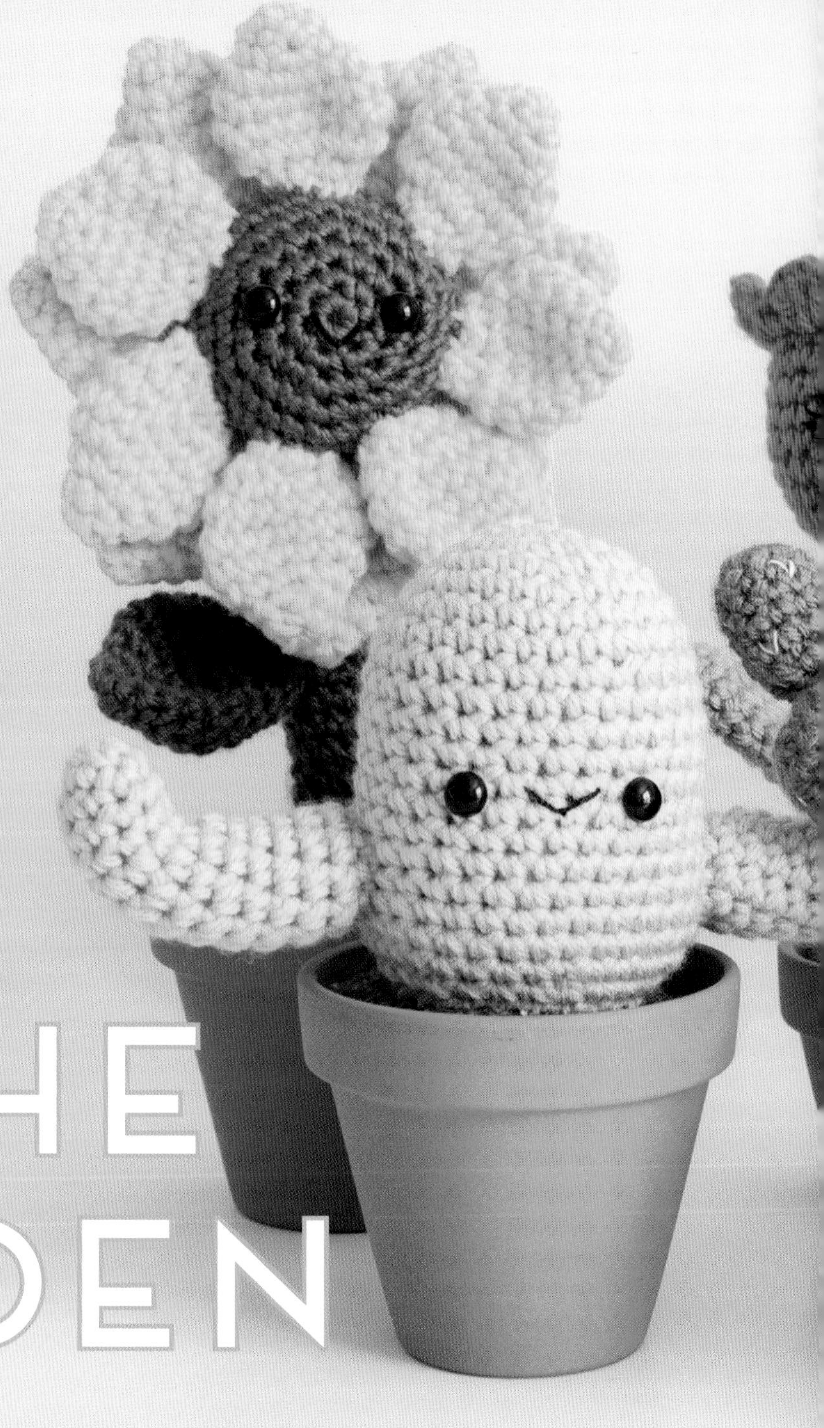

SAGUARO CACTUS

FINISHED MEASUREMENTS
- X Approx. 7 inches tall by 6.5 inches wide

MATERIALS
- X Worsted weight yarn: green and brown
- X Size G/4.25mm crochet hook
- X Pair of 9mm safety eyes
- X Black embroidery floss and small embroidery needle
- X Polyester fiberfill stuffing
- X Yarn needle
- X 3" terra cotta pot
- X Hot glue gun
- X Small piece of brown felt
- X Scissors
- X Stitch marker
- X Straight pins (optional, but very helpful when assembling the arms)

ABBREVIATIONS
- X Mr – Magic ring
- X R – Round
- X Sc – Single crochet
- X Sts – Stitches
- X Inv Dec – Invisible decrease
- X Sl St – Slip stitch

PATTERN NOTES
- X This pattern is crocheted in continuous rounds
- X Crochet all the pieces one at time, and then assemble

CACTUS

BODY

Using green yarn,

Round 1: 6 sc in magic ring (6 sts)
R2: 2 sc in each st around. (12 sts)
R3: *Sc 1, 2 sc in next st,* 6 times. (18 sts)
R4: *Sc 2, 2 sc in next st,* 6 times. (24 sts)
R5: *Sc 3, 2 sc in next st,* 6 times. (30 sts)
R6-19: Sc 30.

Add safety eyes and stitch mouth.

R20: *Sc 3, inv dec 1, * 6 times. (24 sts)

Stuff cactus. Fasten off and leave a tail for sewing.

ARMS: MAKE 2

Using green yarn,

Round 1: 5 sc in magic ring (5 sts)
R2: 2 sc in each st around. (10 sts)
R3-13: Sc 10.

Stuff arms. Fasten off and leave a tail for sewing.

TO BEND ARMS:

Cut a length of green yarn and tie a knot at one end. With the yarn needle, insert into one of the holes on the side of the arm. Pull needle through the middle of one of the stitches between rounds 6 and 7 (photo 1). Insert the needle into the stitch directly below (photo 2) and pull out through another hole in the side of the arm (photo 3). Gently pull the yarn and the arm will bend (photo 4). Tie off and weave in end.

DIRT

Using brown yarn,

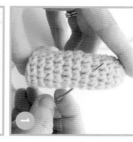

Round 1: 6 sc in magic ring (6 sts)
R2: 2 sc in each st around. (12 sts)
R3: *Sc 1, 2 sc in next st,* 6 times. (18 sts)
R4: *Sc 2, 2 sc in next st,* 6 times. (24 sts)
R5: *Sc 3, 2 sc in next st,* 6 times. (30 sts)
R6: *Sc 4, 2 sc in next st,* 6 times. (36 sts)
R7: *Sc 5, 2 sc in next st,* 6 times. (42 sts)
R8: Sc 42 through **BACK** loops ONLY.

Fasten off.

ASSEMBLY

1. Attach the arms to the side of cactus with straight pins. Sew to the body using a yarn needle. Sew the cactus body to the dirt (photo 1).

2. With hot glue gun, glue a small piece of brown felt over the hole in the bottom of the pot (photo 2). This step is optional if your pot does not have a hole. I like to cover this up by adding felt to make it look like dirt and to hide the fiberfill in step 4.

3. Place some fiber-fill inside of pot (photo 3).

4. To attach the cactus to the pot, begin at the back and place glue along the "lip" of the dirt (photo 4), add a little bit at a time and press onto the pot. (The "lip" is round 8 where we crocheted through the back loops in the dirt section.) It works well to use a chopstick to gently push through the stitches to make sure the glue dries and attaches to the pot (photo 5).

5. Continue adding glue and pressing until you have reached the end (photo 6).

SUCCULENT PLANTER

FINISHED MEASUREMENTS

X Approx. 8 inches tall by 5 inches wide

MATERIALS

X Worsted weight yarn: variety of greens, brown, taupe
X Size G/4.25mm crochet hook
X 2 pairs of 9mm safety eyes
X Black and white embroidery floss and small embroidery needle
X Polyester fiberfill stuffing
X Cardboard
X Yarn needle
X Scissors
X Stitch marker
X Straight pins (optional, but very helpful when assembling the pieces)

ABBREVIATIONS

X Mr - Magic ring
X Ch - Chain
X R - Round
X Sc - Single crochet
X Dc - Double crochet
X Sts - Stitches
X Inv Dec - Invisible decrease
X Sl St - Slip stitch

PATTERN NOTES

X This pattern is crocheted in continuous rounds

POT

Using taupe yarn,

Round 1: 6 sc in magic ring (6 sts)
R2: 2 sc in each st around. (12 sts)
R3: *Sc 1, 2 sc in next st,* 6 times. (18 sts)
R4: *Sc 2, 2 sc in next st,* 6 times. (24 sts)
R5: *Sc 3, 2 sc in next st,* 6 times. (30 sts)
R6: *Sc 4, 2 sc in next st,* 6 times. (36 sts)
R7: *Sc 5, 2 sc in next st,* 6 times. (42 sts)
R8: *Sc 6, 2 sc in next st,* 6 times. (48 sts)
R9: *Sc 7, 2 sc in next st,* 6 times. (54 sts)
R10: *Sc 8, 2 sc in next st,* 6 times. (60 sts)
R11: Sc 60 through **BACK** loops only.
R12-20: Sc 60.
R21: Sc 60 through **FRONT** loops only.
R22: Sc 60 through **BACK** loops only.

Fasten off and weave in ends.

With cardboard, trace around the base of pot and cut out. Place cardboard circle in base of pot *(photo 1).*

DIRT

Using brown yarn,

Round 1: 6 sc in magic ring (6 sts)
R2: 2 sc in each st around. (12 sts)
R3: *Sc 1, 2 sc in next st,* 6 times. (18 sts)
R4: *Sc 2, 2 sc in next st,* 6 times. (24 sts)
R5: *Sc 3, 2 sc in next st,* 6 times. (30 sts)
R6: *Sc 4, 2 sc in next st,* 6 times. (36 sts)
R7: *Sc 5, 2 sc in next st,* 6 times. (42 sts)
R8: *Sc 6, 2 sc in next st,* 6 times. (48 sts)
R9: *Sc 7, 2 sc in next st,* 6 times. (54 sts)
R10: *Sc 8, 2 sc in next st,* 6 times. (60 sts)

Fasten off and leave an extra long tail for sewing.

Set aside.

PRICKLY PEAR CACTUS

MAIN CACTUS PIECE: MAKE 1
Using green yarn,

Round 1: 6 sc in magic ring (6 sts)
R2: 2 sc in each st around. (12 sts)
R3: *Sc 1, 2 sc in next st,* 6 times. (18 sts)
R4: *Sc 2, 2 sc in next st,* 6 times. (24 sts)
R5: *Sc 3, 2 sc in next st,* 6 times. (30 sts)
R6-12: Sc 30.

Add safety eyes and stitch mouth.

R13: *Sc 3, inv dec 1,* 6 times. (24 sts)
R14-15: Sc 24.
R16: *Sc 2, inv dec 1,* 6 times. (18 sts)
R17-18: Sc 18.

Stuff cactus. Fasten off and leave a tail for sewing.

MEDIUM CACTUS PIECE: MAKE 1
Using green yarn,

Round 1: 6 sc in magic ring (6 sts)
R2: 2 sc in each st around. (12 sts)
R3: *Sc 1, 2 sc in next st,* 6 times. (18 sts)
R4-5: Sc 18.
R6: *Sc 1, inv dec 1,* 6 times. (12 sts)
R7-8: Sc 12.

Stuff cactus. Fasten off and leave a tail for sewing.

SMALL CACTUS PIECE: MAKE 2
Using green yarn,

Round 1: 6 sc in magic ring (6 sts)
R2: 2 sc in each st around. (12 sts)
R3-6: Sc 12.
R7: *Sc 1, inv dec 1,* 4 times. (8 sts)

Stuff cactus. Fasten off and leave a tail for sewing.

FOR THE WHITE PRICKLES:
With white embroidery floss (divided into 3 strands) stitch a "V" in various places.

TO ASSEMBLE:
Take one small cactus piece and sew onto the medium cactus. Next, sew the medium cactus piece onto the main cactus. Sew the last small cactus to the main cactus piece.

BARREL CACTUS

Using green yarn, Ch 9

Row 1: Sc in 2nd ch from hook and in each ch across, 8 stitches total. Ch 1 and turn.

Row 2-21: Sc in **FRONT** loops only, in each sc across, 8 stitches total. Ch 1 and turn.

Fasten off and leave a long tail for sewing. Add safety eyes and stitch mouth (photo 1).

To sew up cactus, weave yarn needle through the top edge of the cactus (photo 2). At the end, pull yarn tight and the top will come together (photo 3). To close the hole more, weave needle through the top (photo 4). Sew down the side of the cactus that is open (photo 5). Leave tail for sewing the cactus to the dirt.

ASSEMBLY

1. Sew prickly pear and barrel cactus onto dirt. Add fiberfill before sewing the barrel cactus on all the way. Sew lady finger cactus behind the barrel cactus and prickly pear *(photo 2)*.

2. Sew 3 strings of pearls along the side, in front of the prickly pear *(photo 3)*. Sew the remaining 2 towards the center of the dirt to fill in the gaps *(photo 4)*.

3. With a yarn needle, sew the dirt to the pot. To create invisible stitching, weave the yarn needle through the last row of stitches on the dirt and the back loops from **R21** on the pot *(photo 5 & 6)*. By doing this, the darker yarn for the dirt will not show on the outside of the pot.

4. Make sure to stuff the pot with fiberfill before closing the hole *(photo 7)*.

SUNFLOWER

FINISHED MEASUREMENTS
- ✕ Approx. 10.5 inches tall by 5.5 inches wide

MATERIALS
- ✕ Worsted weight yarn: yellow, chestnut brown, green, and brown
- ✕ Size G/4.25mm crochet hook
- ✕ Pair of 9mm safety eyes
- ✕ Black embroidery floss and small embroidery needle
- ✕ Polyester fiberfill stuffing
- ✕ Yarn needle
- ✕ 3" terra cotta pot
- ✕ Hot glue gun
- ✕ 7.5 inch wooden dowel (3/8 inch thickness)
- ✕ Small piece of cardboard
- ✕ Small piece of brown felt
- ✕ Scissors
- ✕ Stitch marker
- ✕ Straight pins (optional, but very helpful when assembling the petals)

ABBREVIATIONS
- ✕ Mr – Magic ring
- ✕ R – Round
- ✕ Sc – Single crochet
- ✕ Sts – Stitches
- ✕ Inv Dec – Invisible decrease
- ✕ Sl St – Slip stitch

PATTERN NOTES
- ✕ This pattern is crocheted in continuous rounds
- ✕ Crochet all the pieces one at a time, and then assemble

FLOWER CENTER

Using chestnut brown yarn (or yellow for daisy),

Round 1: 6 sc in magic ring (6 sts)
R2: 2 sc in each st around. (12 sts)
R3: *Sc 1, 2 sc in next st,* 6 times. (18 sts)
R4: *Sc 2, 2 sc in next st,* 6 times. (24 sts)
R5: *Sc 3, 2 sc in next st,* 6 times. (30 sts)

Add safety eyes and stitch mouth.

R6-8: Sc 30.
R9: *Sc 3, inv dec 1,* 6 times. (24 sts)
R10: *Sc 2, inv dec 1,* 6 times. (18 sts)
R11: *Sc 1, inv dec 1,* 6 times. (12 sts)

Begin stuffing and continue as you close up the center.

R12: Inv dec around 6 times. (6 sts)

Fasten off and close piece.

PETALS: MAKE 14

Using yellow yarn,

Round 1: 5 sc in magic ring (5 sts)
R2: Sc 5.
R3: 2 sc in each st around. (10 sts)
R4: *Sc 1, 2 sc in next st,* 5 times. (15 sts)
R5-6: Sc 15.
R7: *Sc 1, inv dec 1,* 5 times (10 sts)
R8: Inv dec around 5 times. (5 sts)

Fasten off and leave a tail for sewing.

DIRT

Using brown yarn,

Round 1: 6 sc in magic ring (6 sts)

Insert the dowel into the middle of magic ring and tighten. You will crochet around the dowel.

R2: 2 sc in each st around. (12 sts)
R3: *Sc 1, 2 sc in next st,* 6 times. (18 sts)
R4: *Sc 2, 2 sc in next st,* 6 times. (24 sts)
R5: *Sc 3, 2 sc in next st,* 6 times. (30 sts)
R6: *Sc 4, 2 sc in next st,* 6 times. (36 sts)
R7: *Sc 5, 2 sc in next st,* 6 times. (42 sts)
R8: Sc 42 through **BACK** loops ONLY.

Fasten off.

STEM

Using green yarn,

Round 1: 5 sc in magic ring (5 sts)
R2: 2 sc in each st around. (10 sts)
R3: Sc 10 in each round until the stem measures 4.5 inches long.

Fasten off and leave a tail for sewing.

BACK CIRCLE

(Goes on top of the stem, on the back of the flower)

Using green yarn,

Round 1: 6 sc in magic ring (6 sts)
R2: 2 sc in each st around. (12 sts)
R3: *Sc 1, 2 sc in next st,* 6 times. (18 sts)
R4: *Sc 2, 2 sc in next st,* 6 times. (24 sts)
R5: Sc 24.

Fasten off and leave a long tail for sewing.

LEAF: MAKE 2

Using green yarn,

Round 1: 6 sc in magic ring
R2: Sc 6.
R3: 2 sc in each st around. (12 sts)
R4: *Sc 1, 2 sc in next st,* 6 times. (18 sts)
R5-6: Sc 18.
R7: *Sc 1, inv dec 1,* 6 times. (12 sts)
R8-10: Sc 12.
R11: Inv dec around 6 times. (6 sts)

Fasten off and leave a tail for sewing.

TO MAKE A DAISY

You will need white yarn for the petals and yellow yarn for the center. Crochet all the same pieces as you would for the sunflower, replacing the petals with the pattern below.

PETALS: MAKE 9

Using white yarn,

Round 1: 6 sc in magic ring (6 sts)
R2: 2 sc in each st around. (12 sts)
R3-5: Sc 12.
R6: *Sc 1, inv dec 1,* 4 times. (8 sts)
R7: Sc 8.
R8: *Sc 1, inv dec 1,* 2 times, sc 1 and sl st into the last st. (5 sts)

Fasten off and leave a tail for sewing.

FLOWER ASSEMBLY

1. Sew the petals to the flower center *(photos 1 & 2)*.

   For sunflower: with straight pins, place 7 petals evenly around the flower center. Sew all 7 petals in place before doing the back row. Place the remaining 7 petals in between the first row of petals. You want to stagger them so the flower looks more full. Sew petals.

   For daisy: with straight pins, place the 9 petals evenly around the flower center and sew in place.

2. Place the stem on the wooden dowel and sew the stem to the dirt *(photo 3)*.

3. Cut a decent length of extra green yarn and tie a knot at one end. Make sure the flower is centered on the stem. Sew the stem to the back of the flower center. Weave the yarn back and forth through the stem and the flower center, making sure it is securely attached *(photos 4-6)*.

4. Sew the back circle on top of the stem *(photo 7 & 8)*.

5. Sew on the leaves on each side of the stem.

ATTACHING TO TERRA COTTA POT

1. With a hot glue gun, glue the cardboard and brown felt together *(photo 9)*. With the cardboard side up, place a large dollop of hot glue and place the dowel in the center of it *(photo 10)*. Place the flower inside the terra cotta pot while the glue cools so the flower stays straight *(photo 11)*. Once the glue has cooled, place some glue inside the pot, around the bottom and place the cardboard base on top of it. Press to secure the flower and pot.

2. Add some fiberfill around the dowel to give it some stability. This also allows the dirt to look like it is piled up around the flower once it is finished. You are now ready to attach the flower to the pot.

3. To attach the flower to the pot, begin at the back and place glue along the "lip" of the dirt, add a little bit at a time and press onto the pot. The "lip" is round 8 where we crocheted through the back loops, in the dirt section. Use a chopstick to gently push through the stitches to make sure the glue attaches and dries to the pot. Continue adding glue and pressing until you have reached the end *(photo 12)*.

TULIP

FINISHED MEASUREMENTS
- ✕ Approx. 8.5 inches tall by 2.5 inches wide

MATERIALS
- ✕ Worsted weight yarn: pink, green, and brown
- ✕ Size G/4.25mm crochet hook
- ✕ Pair of 9mm safety eyes
- ✕ Black embroidery floss and small embroidery needle
- ✕ Polyester fiberfill stuffing
- ✕ 2" terra cotta pot
- ✕ Three (3) 12 inch pipe cleaners (or "chenille stems")
- ✕ Yarn needle
- ✕ Scissors
- ✕ Stitch marker

ABBREVIATIONS
- ✕ Mr – Magic ring
- ✕ R – Round
- ✕ Sc – Single crochet
- ✕ Dc – Double crochet
- ✕ Tr – Triple crochet
- ✕ Sts – Stitches
- ✕ Inv Dec – Invisible decrease
- ✕ Sl St – Slip stitch

PATTERN NOTES
- ✕ This pattern is crocheted in continuous rounds
- ✕ The flower is assembled as you go

FLOWER CENTER: MAKE 1

Using pink yarn,

Round 1: 6 sc in magic ring (6 sts)
R2: 2 sc in each st around. (12 sts)
R3: *Sc 1, 2 sc in next st,* 6 times. (18 sts)
R4: *Sc 2, 2 sc in next st,* 6 times. (24 sts)
R5: *Sc 3, 2 sc in next st,* 6 times. (30 sts)

Fasten off and leave a long tail for sewing. Set aside.

FLOWER

Using pink yarn,

Round 1: 6 sc in magic ring (6 sts)
R2: 2 sc in each st around. (12 sts)
R3: *Sc 1, 2 sc in next st,* 6 times. (18 sts)
R4: *Sc 2, 2 sc in next st,* 6 times. (24 sts)
R5: *Sc 3, 2 sc in next st,* 6 times. (30 sts)
R6-13: Sc 30.
R14: *dc, tr, dc in one stitch, sc 2,* 10 times. (50 sts)

Fasten off and weave in the end.

Add safety eyes, stitch mouth and eyelashes.

STEM

Using green yarn,

Round 1: 7 sc in magic ring (7 sts)
R2-14: Sc 7.

After you've crocheted round 3, fold 3 pipe cleaners in half *(photo 1)*. Insert the tips of the pipe cleaners into the magic ring hole, pulling through about 1.5 inches *(photo 2)*. Crochet around the pipe cleaners until you've finished round 14 *(photo 3)*.

Fasten off and leave a tail for sewing.

Take the flower base and insert the pipe cleaners into the magic ring hole *(photo 4)*. You'll insert 6 ends total into the flower base. Twist ends together. Sew the stem to the flower with green yarn and tie off *(photo 5)*.

Stuff flower and sew the flower center to the top of the flower. Weave yarn needle through the horizontal stitches just below round 14 from the flower *(photos 6 & 7)*.

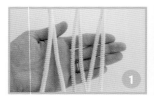

DIRT

Using brown yarn,

Round 1: 6 sc in magic ring (6 sts)
R2: 2 sc in each st around. (12 sts)
R3: *Sc 1, 2 sc in next st,* 6 times. (18 sts)
R4: *Sc 2, 2 sc in next st,* 6 times. (24 sts)
R5: *Sc 3, 2 sc in next st,* 6 times. (30 sts)

Insert the remaining ends of the pipe cleaners into the magic ring hole. With green yarn, sew the stem to dirt *(photo 8)*.

R6-7: Sc 30.
R8: *Sc 3, inv dec 1,* 6 times. (24 sts)
R9: Sc 24.
R10: *Sc 2, inv dec 1,* 6 times. (18 sts)
R11-12: Sc 18.

Stuff and continue as you work.

R13: *Sc 1, inv dec 1,* 6 times. (12 sts)
R14: Inv dec around 6 times. (6 sts)

Fasten off and close piece.

LEAF: MAKE 2

Using green yarn,

Round 1: 4 sc in magic ring (4 sts)
R2: 2 sc in each st around. (8 sts)
R3-14: Sc 8.
R15: Inv dec around 4 times. (4 sts)

Fasten off and leave a tail for sewing.

Attach leaves on either side of the stem, sewing into the dirt and up the stem about ½ an inch *(photo 9)*.

AT THE
AQUARIUM

JELLYFISH

FINISHED MEASUREMENTS
- ✕ Approx. 7 inches tall by 3.5 inches wide

MATERIALS
- ✕ Worsted weight yarn: light green and dark green
- ✕ Size G/4.25mm crochet hook
- ✕ Pair of 9mm safety eyes
- ✕ Black embroidery floss and small embroidery needle
- ✕ Polyester fiberfill stuffing
- ✕ Yarn needle
- ✕ Scissors
- ✕ Stitch marker

ABBREVIATIONS
- ✕ Mr – Magic ring
- ✕ R – Round
- ✕ Sc – Single crochet
- ✕ Sts – Stitches
- ✕ Inv Dec – Invisible decrease
- ✕ Hdc – Half double crochet
- ✕ Sl St – Slip stitch
- ✕ Ch – Chain

PATTERN NOTES
- ✕ This pattern is crocheted in continuous rounds

BODY

Using light green yarn,

Round 1: 6 sc in magic ring (6 sts)
R2: 2 sc in each st around. (12 sts)
R3: *Sc 1, 2 sc in next st,* 6 times. (18 sts)
R4: *Sc 2, 2 sc in next st,* 6 times. (24 sts)
R5: *Sc 3, 2 sc in next st,* 6 times. (30 sts)
R6: *Sc 4, 2 sc in next st,* 6 times. (36 sts)
R7: *Sc 5, 2 sc in next st,* 6 times. (42 sts)
R8–14: Sc 42.
R15: Through **FRONT** loops only, *Sc 1, hdc 1, sc 1 in one st, sc 1 in next st,* 21 times. (84 sts)
Sl st and fasten off.

Add safety eyes and stitch mouth *(photo 1)*.

BELLY

Using dark green yarn,

Round 1: 6 sc in magic ring (6 sts)
R2: 2 sc in each st around. (12 sts)
R3: *Sc 1, 2 sc in next st,* 6 times. (18 sts)
R4: *Sc 2, 2 sc in next st,* 6 times. (24 sts)
R5: *Sc 3, 2 sc in next st,* 6 times. (30 sts)
R6: *Sc 4, 2 sc in next st,* 6 times. (36 sts)
R7: *Sc 5, 2 sc in next st,* 6 times. (42 sts)

Fasten off and leave a tail for sewing *(photo 2)*.

TENTACLES: 18 TOTAL

THICK TENTACLES: MAKE 10 (5 of each color) *(photo 3)*
Ch 30, then sl st in 2nd ch from hook and in each ch across (29 total).

Fasten off and leave a tail.

SKINNY TENTACLES: MAKE 8 (5 dark green, 3 light green) *(photo 4)*
Ch 24 and fasten off. Leave a tail.

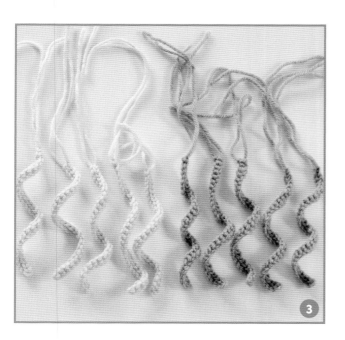

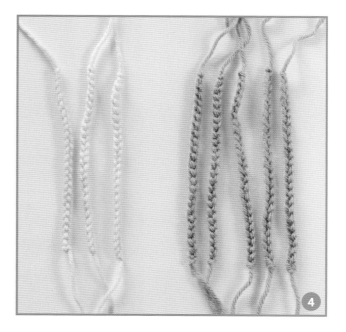

JELLYFISH ASSEMBLY

ATTACHING TENTACLES (working from the center of the belly):

1. Attach the 3 skinny light green tentacles evenly around the magic ring of the belly *(photo 1)*.

2. Next, attach 5 of the thick dark green tentacles, placing them evenly around the 3 skinny ones *(photo 2)*.

3. Place the remaining 5 thick light green tentacles evenly around the belly (about 2 rows from the edge of the belly, *photo 3*).

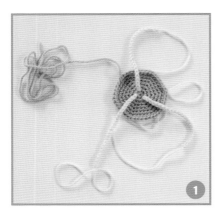

4. Attach the 5 remaining skinny dark green tentacles, positioning them in the middle of the thick light green tentacles *(photo 4)*.

5. Make sure to securely knot the loose strands on the inside of the belly. Trim strands *(photo 5)*.

TO FINISH THE JELLYFISH:

1. To attach the belly to the body of the jellyfish, weave the yarn needle through the last row of stitches on the belly and the back loops from R15 on the body *(photos 6-9)*.
2. Stuff with fiberfill before closing.

OPTIONAL:

If you would like to have a hanging jellyfish, simply make one more skinny tentacle. With a yarn needle, insert it into a stitch by the magic ring and bring out on the opposite side *(photos 10 & 11)*. Tie a knot on the tail ends and trim ends *(photo 12)*. Then gently pull chain through so that the knot is hidden inside the body *(photos 13 & 14)*.

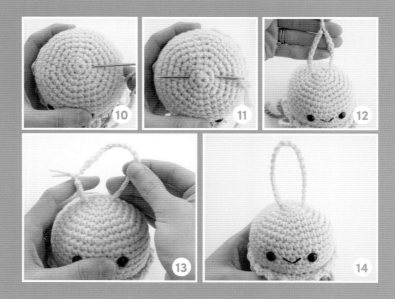

OCTOPUS

FINISHED MEASUREMENTS
- ✕ Approx. 7 inches tall by 3.5 inches wide

MATERIALS
- ✕ Worsted weight yarn: magenta and pink
- ✕ Size G/4.25mm crochet hook
- ✕ Pair of 9mm safety eyes
- ✕ Black embroidery floss and small embroidery needle
- ✕ Polyester fiberfill stuffing
- ✕ Yarn needle
- ✕ Scissors
- ✕ Stitch marker
- ✕ Straight pins (optional but very helpful when assembling the arms)

ABBREVIATIONS
- ✕ Mr – Magic ring
- ✕ R – Round
- ✕ Sc – Single crochet
- ✕ Sts – Stitches
- ✕ Inv Dec – Invisible decrease
- ✕ Sl St – Slip stitch

PATTERN NOTES
- ✕ This pattern is crocheted in continuous rounds

EYE SOCKETS: MAKE 2

Using pink yarn,

Round 1: 4 sc in magic ring (4 sts)
R2: 2 sc in each st around. (8 sts)
R3: *Sc 1, 2 sc in next st,* 4 times. (12 sts)

Fasten off and leave a tail for sewing. Place a safety eye between round 1 and 2, leave backing off *(photo 1).*

Set aside.

BODY

Using magenta yarn,

Round 1: 6 sc in magic ring (6 sts)
R2: 2 sc in each st around. (12 sts)
R3: *Sc 1, 2 sc in next st,* 6 times. (18 sts)
R4: *Sc 2, 2 sc in next st,* 6 times. (24 sts)
R5: *Sc 3, 2 sc in next st,* 6 times. (30 sts)
R6: *Sc 4, 2 sc in next st,* 6 times. (36 sts)

R7: *Sc 5, 2 sc in next st,* 6 times. (42 sts)
R8-18: Sc 42.

Attach the eye sockets *(photo 2).* Weave in the tail from the start of the magic ring, then sew the socket on with the ending tail. Add safety backing. Leave a space in between for sewing on the mouth *(photo 3).*

R19: Through **BACK** loops only, *Sc 5, inv dec 1,* 6 times. (36 sts)
R20: *Sc 4, inv dec 1,* 6 times. (30 sts)
R21: *Sc 3, inv dec 1,* 6 times. (24 sts)
R22: *Sc 2, inv dec 1,* 6 times. (18 sts)

Stuff body.

R23: *Sc 1, inv dec 1,* 6 times. (12 sts)
R24: Inv dec around 6 times. (6 sts)

Fasten off and close piece.

ARMS: MAKE 8

Using magenta yarn,

Round 1: 4 sc in magic ring (4 sts)
R2: 2 sc in each st around. (8 sts)
R3-16: Sc 8. Add fiberfill as you go.

Fasten off and leave a tail for sewing.

Sew the arms around the edge of the body. Make sure to space them evenly so they all fit *(photos 5-8)*.

TURTLE

FINISHED MEASUREMENTS
- ✕ Approx. 6.5 inches long by 7 inches wide

MATERIALS
- ✕ Worsted weight yarn: green, dark brown, light brown, and tan
- ✕ Size G/4.25mm crochet hook
- ✕ Pair of 9mm safety eyes
- ✕ Black embroidery floss and small embroidery needle
- ✕ Polyester fiberfill stuffing
- ✕ Yarn needle
- ✕ Scissors
- ✕ Stitch marker

ABBREVIATIONS
- ✕ Mr – Magic ring
- ✕ R – Round
- ✕ Sc – Single crochet
- ✕ Sts – Stitches
- ✕ Inv Dec – Invisible decrease
- ✕ Sl St – Slip stitch

PATTERN NOTES
- ✕ This pattern is crocheted in continuous rounds

BELLY

Using tan yarn,

Round 1: 6 sc in magic ring (6 sts)
R2: 2 sc in each st around. (12 sts)
R3: *Sc 1, 2 sc in next st,* 6 times. (18 sts)
R4: *Sc 2, 2 sc in next st,* 6 times. (24 sts)
R5: *Sc 3, 2 sc in next st,* 6 times. (30 sts)
R6: *Sc 4, 2 sc in next st,* 6 times. (36 sts)
R7: *Sc 5, 2 sc in next st,* 6 times. (42 sts)
R8: *Sc 6, 2 sc in next st,* 6 times. (48 sts)
R9: *Sc 7, 2 sc in next st,* 6 times. (54 sts)

Fasten off and leave a long tail for sewing.

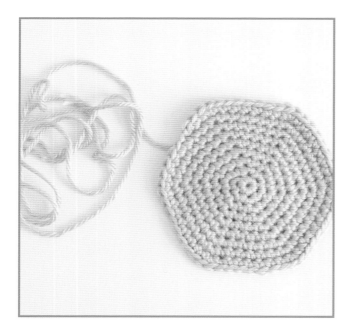

HEAD

Using green yarn,

Round 1: 6 sc in magic ring (6 sts)
R2: 2 sc in each st around. (12 sts)
R3: *Sc 1, 2 sc in next st,* 6 times. (18 sts)
R4: *Sc 2, 2 sc in next st,* 6 times. (24 sts)
R5: *Sc 3, 2 sc in next st,* 6 times. (30 sts)
R6-10: Sc 30.
R11: *Sc 3, inv dec 1,* 6 times. (24 sts)

Add safety eyes and stitch mouth. For the nose, make two little knots above the mouth.

R12: *Sc 2, inv dec 1,* 6 times. (18 sts)
R13: *Sc 1, inv dec 1,* 6 times. (12 sts)

Stuff head.

R14: Inv dec around 6 times. (6 sts)

Fasten off and close piece.

FRONT LEGS: MAKE 2

Using green yarn,

Round 1: 6 sc in magic ring (6 sts)
R2: 2 sc in each st around. (12 sts)
R3: Sc 12.
R4: *Sc 1, 2 sc in next st,* 6 times. (18 sts)
R5-7: Sc 18.
R8: *Sc 1, inv dec 1,* 6 times. (12 sts)
R9: Sc 12.
R10: *Sc 1, inv dec 1,* 4 times. (8 sts)

Fasten off and trim tail. Add a little bit of stuffing.

BACK LEGS: MAKE 2

Using green yarn,

Round 1: 5 sc in magic ring (5 sts)
R2: 2 sc in each st around. (10 sts)
R3: Sc 10.
R4: *Sc 1, 2 sc in next st,* 5 times. (15 sts)
R5-7: Sc 15.
R8: *Sc 1, inv dec 1,* 5 times. (10 sts)
R9: Sc 10.
R10: *Sc 1, inv dec 1,* 3 times, sl st in last stitch. (7 sts)

Fasten off and trim tail. Add a little bit of stuffing.

SHELL

Using dark brown yarn,

Round 1: 6 sc in magic ring (6 sts)
R2: 2 sc in each st around. (12 sts)
R3: *Sc 1, 2 sc in next st,* 6 times. (18 sts)
R4: *Sc 2, 2 sc in next st,* 6 times. (24 sts)
R5: *Sc 3, 2 sc in next st,* 6 times. (30 sts)
R6: *Sc 4, 2 sc in next st,* 6 times. (36 sts)
R7: *Sc 5, 2 sc in next st,* 6 times. (42 sts)
R8: *Sc 6, 2 sc in next st,* 6 times. (48 sts)
R9: *Sc 7, 2 sc in next st,* 6 times. (54 sts)
R10-19: Sc 54.
R20: Sc 54 through **FRONT** loops only.
R21: Sc 54.

Fasten off and weave in end.

FOR SHELL DETAIL:

1. With light brown yarn and a yarn needle, back stitch a hexagon between rounds 5 and 6 *(photo 1)*.

2. Next, count 8 rows down until you reach rounds 13 and 14. Back stitch a straight line around the whole shell and tie off *(photo 2)*.

3. On each point of the hexagon, back stitch a line on a slight angle, about 4 stitches. Then turn and back stitch down until you reach the straight line *(photo 3)*. We're essentially making a wide V shape that is on its side. Make sure that every other line is the opposite, almost like making another hexagon in between the straight line and original hexagon *(photos 4 & 5)*.

4. For the last row, repeat the steps for making another slight angle, this time going below the straight line. Make sure every other line is opposite like in step 3. Back stitch lines and make sure to stop where **R20** from the shell begins *(photos 6 & 7)*.

TURTLE ASSEMBLY

1. With green yarn and a yarn needle, sew the turtle head to the shell. Place the head about 2 rows above **R20** from the shell *(photo 1)*.

2. Place the front legs at the top of the belly on the corners, leaving one side open in between them *(photo 2)*. With tan yarn, sew legs to the belly with a back stitch. Make sure to sew them on the inside of the body *(the part that won't be showing, photos 3 & 4)*.

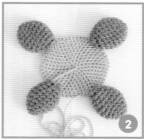

3. Repeat for the back legs, this time working on the bottom half of the body. Leave one side open between the back legs, just like the front legs *(photo 5)*.

4. To attach the belly to the shell, first make sure the head is centered between the front legs *(photo 6)*. With tan yarn, begin to weave the yarn needle back and forth through the belly and shell. To create invisible stitching while sewing, weave the yarn needle through the last row of stitches on the belly and the back loops from **R20** on the shell *(photos 7 & 8)*. When you reach the legs, do the same technique but this time the leg will be included *(photos 9-11)*.

5. Make sure to stuff the shell with fiberfill before closing up the hole *(photos 12 & 13)*.

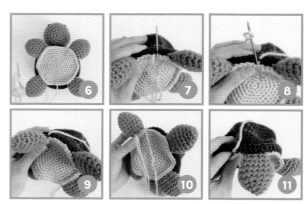

WHALE

FINISHED MEASUREMENTS

✗ Approx. 9 inches long by 4 inches wide (7 inches from fin to fin)

MATERIALS

✗ Worsted weight yarn: aqua. If making a narwhal, you'll need white for the tusk.
✗ Size G/4.25mm crochet hook
✗ Pair of 12mm safety eyes
✗ Black embroidery floss and small embroidery needle
✗ Polyester fiberfill stuffing
✗ Yarn needle
✗ Scissors
✗ Stitch marker
✗ Straight pins (optional, but very helpful when assembling the fins)

ABBREVIATIONS

✗ Mr – Magic ring
✗ R – Round
✗ Sc – Single crochet
✗ Sts – Stitches
✗ Inv Dec – Invisible decrease
✗ Sl St – Slip stitch

PATTERN NOTES

✗ This pattern is crocheted in continuous rounds

BODY

Using aqua yarn,

Round 1: 6 sc in magic ring (6 sts)
R2: 2 sc in each st around. (12 sts)
R3: *Sc 1, 2 sc in next st,* 6 times. (18 sts)
R4: *Sc 2, 2 sc in next st,* 6 times. (24 sts)
R5: *Sc 3, 2 sc in next st,* 6 times. (30 sts)
R6: *Sc 4, 2 sc in next st,* 6 times. (36 sts)
R7: *Sc 5, 2 sc in next st,* 6 times. (42 sts)
R8: *Sc 6, 2 sc in next st,* 6 times. (48 sts)
R9: *Sc 7, 2 sc in next st,* 6 times. (54 sts)
R10–21: Sc 54.

For the eyes: first place the right eye (your left) between rounds 12 and 13 from magic ring *(photo 1)*. For the left eye (your right) count 25 stitches around the bottom of the whale, over to the right *(photos 2 & 3)*.

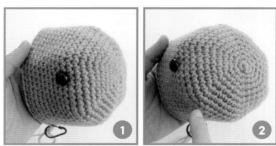

For the mouth: with black embroidery floss, back stitch from 2 sts below one eye across to the other eye, leaving two sts *(photos 4–6)*.

R22: *Sc 7, inv dec 1,* 6 times. (48 sts)
R23: *Sc 6, inv dec 1,* 6 times. (42 sts)
R24–25: Sc 42.
R26: *Sc 5, inv dec 1,* 6 times. (36 sts)
R27–28: Sc 36.
R29: *Sc 4, inv dec 1,* 6 times. (30 sts)

Start stuffing and continue as you go.

R30–32: Sc 30.
R33: *Sc 3, inv dec 1,* 6 times. (24 sts)
R34–35: Sc 24.
R36: *Sc 2, inv dec 1,* 6 times. (18 sts)
R37–40: Sc 18.
R41: *Sc 1, inv dec 1,* 6 times. (12 sts)
R42–44: Sc 12.

Fasten off and leave a tail for sewing. Flatten tail and sew closed *(photos 7 & 8)*.

FINS AND TAIL: MAKE 4

Using aqua yarn,

Round 1: 5 sc in magic ring (5 sts)
R2: 2 sc in each st around. (10 sts)
R3: Sc 10.
R4: *Sc 1, 2 sc in next st,* 5 times. (15 sts)
R5-7: Sc 15.
R8: *Sc 1, inv dec 1,* 5 times. (10 sts)
R9: Sc 10.

Fasten off and leave a tail for sewing.

For the tail: Place the the fins evenly on the tail, part of the fin will hang off and need to be sewn to the side of the tail *(photos 9 & 10)*.

Sew the remaining two fins on the sides of the body *(photos 11-13)*.

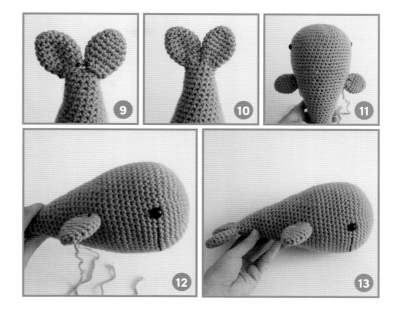

TO MAKE A NARWHAL: TUSK

Using white yarn,

Round 1: 5 sc in magic ring (5 sts)
R2: Sc 5.
R3: 2 sc in each st around. (10 sts)
R4-14: Sc 10.

Add fiberfill to tusk.

Fasten off and leave a tail for sewing. Position and sew tusk between the eyes *(photos 14 & 15)*.

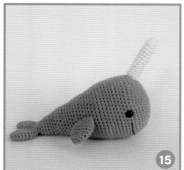

DOWN ON THE FARM

FINISHED MEASUREMENTS

- ✗ Bunny – Approx. 9 inches tall by 3.5 inches wide
- ✗ Carrot – Approx. 4.5 inches tall by 1 inch wide

MATERIALS

- ✗ Worsted weight yarn:
  - Bunny – gray and pink
  - Carrot – orange and green
- ✗ Size G/4.25mm crochet hook
- ✗ Pair of 9mm safety eyes for bunny
- ✗ Pair of 6mm safety eyes for carrot
- ✗ Embroidery floss that matches the color you picked for the bunny
- ✗ Black embroidery floss – for carrot mouth
- ✗ Small embroidery needle
- ✗ Gray felt (optional; can be used for the belly)
- ✗ Polyester fiberfill stuffing
- ✗ Yarn needle
- ✗ Scissors
- ✗ Stitch marker
- ✗ Straight pins (optional, but very helpful when assembling the pieces)

ABBREVIATIONS

- ✗ Mr – Magic ring
- ✗ R – Round
- ✗ Sc – Single crochet
- ✗ Sts – Stitches
- ✗ Inv Dec – Invisible decrease
- ✗ Sl St – Slip stitch

PATTERN NOTES

- ✗ This pattern is crocheted in continuous rounds

HEAD

Using gray yarn,

Round 1: 6 sc in magic ring (6 sts)
R2: 2 sc in each st around. (12 sts)
R3: *Sc 1, 2 sc in next st,* 6 times. (18 sts)
R4: *Sc 2, 2 sc in next st,* 6 times. (24 sts)
R5: *Sc 3, 2 sc in next st,* 6 times. (30 sts)
R6: *Sc 4, 2 sc in next st,* 6 times. (36 sts)
R7-12: Sc 36.

Add safety eyes.

For the nose — using embroidery floss in desired color, satin stitch a small nose between the eyes. Once done, make one line going vertically for the mouth (photo 1).

R13: *Sc 4, inv dec 1,* 6 times. (30 sts)
R14: *Sc 3, inv dec 1,* 6 times. (24 sts)
R15: *Sc 2, inv dec 1,* 6 times. (18 sts)

Begin stuffing with fiberfill and continue as you go.

R16: *Sc 1, inv dec 1,* 6 times. (12 sts)
R17: Inv dec around 6 times. (6 sts)

Fasten off and close piece.

EARS: MAKE 2

Using gray yarn,

Round 1: 5 sc in magic ring (5 sts)
R2: 2 sc in each st around. (10 sts)
R3: *Sc 1, 2 sc in next st,* 5 times. (15 sts)
R4-7: Sc 15.
R8: *Sc 1, inv dec 1,* 5 times. (10 sts)
R9-12: Sc 10.

Fasten off and leave a tail for sewing. Flatten pieces before positioning and sewing to head (photos 2 & 3).

TAIL

Using pink yarn,

Round 1: 5 sc in magic ring (5 sts)
R2: 2 sc in each st around. (10 sts)
R3: Sc 10.

Fasten off and leave a tail for sewing

Set aside.

ARMS: MAKE 2

Using pink yarn,

Round 1: 5 sc in magic ring (5 sts)
R2: 2 sc in each st around. (10 sts)
R3: Sc 10.

Change to gray yarn,

R4-13: Sc 10.

Fasten off and leave a tail for sewing.

Stuff with fiberfill. Set aside.

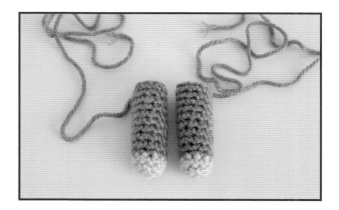

LEGS AND BODY

Using pink yarn,

Round 1: 6 sc in magic ring (6 sts)
R2: 2 sc in each st around. (12 sts)
R3: Sc 12.

Change to gray yarn,

R4-11: Sc 12.

Fasten off and stuff with fiberfill.

Crochet one more leg but do not fasten off *(photo 1)*. With the second leg still on hook, insert hook into the last st of the first leg *(photo 2)*. Sc in each of the stitches of the first leg (12 sts) and then in the second leg *(photos 3 & 4)*. You will have a total of 24 sts at the end. With the tail from the first leg, use it to close up the hole between the two legs *(photos 5-9)*.

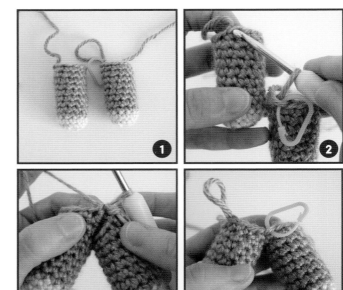

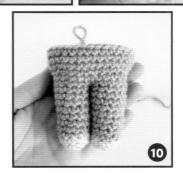

Continue with the following rounds.

R12-13: Sc 24.
R14: *Sc 3, 2 sc in next st,* 6 times. (30 sts)
R15-19: Sc 30.

Begin stuffing with fiberfill and continue as you go *(photo 10)*.

R20: *Sc 3, inv dec 1,* 6 times. (24 sts)
R21: Sc 24.
R22: *Sc 2, inv dec 1,* 6 times. (18 sts)
R23–26: Sc 18.
R27: *Sc 1, inv dec 1,* 6 times. (12 sts)

Fasten off and leave a tail for sewing *(photo 11)*.

TO ADD A FELT BELLY:

1. Cut paper to match the size of your belly *(photo 12)*. Then cut out a piece of gray felt *(photo 13)*.

2. With colored embroidery floss, stitch felt onto body *(photos 14–16)*.

 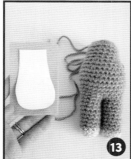   

ASSEMBLY

1. Position head onto body and sew together *(photo 17)*.

2. Position arms on the sides of body. Position tail to back of body. Sew pieces in place *(photo 18)*.

GREEN TOPS: MAKE 6

Using green yarn,

Ch 9, then in 2nd ch from hook sl st in each ch across. (8 total)

Fasten off and leave a tail for sewing (photo 1).

CARROT

Using orange yarn,

Round 1: 6 sc in magic ring (6 sts)
R2: 2 sc in each st around. (12 sts)
R3: *Sc 1, 2 sc in next st,* 6 times. (18 sts)

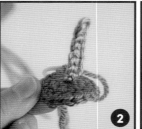

Add green tops. Use a yarn needle to weave the green tails through the top of the carrot (photo 2). Secure with a knot and trim the green ends (photos 3 & 4).

R4-7: Sc 18.
R8: *Sc 4, inv dec 1,* 3 times. (15 sts)
R9-11: Sc 15.

Add safety eyes and stitch mouth.

Begin stuffing with fiberfill and continue as you go.

R12: *Sc 3, inv dec 1,* 3 times. (12 sts)
R13-15: Sc 12.
R16: *Sc 2, inv dec 1,* 3 times. (9 sts)
R17-18: Sc 9.
R19: *Inv dec 1,* 4 times, sl st into last sc. (5 sts)

Fasten off and close piece (photo 5).

CARROT HANDLE: MAKE 1

If you would like the bunny to hold the carrot, make this piece.

Using orange yarn,

Ch 12.

Fasten off and leave a tail for sewing. Sew both ends to the back of carrot, making sure the bunny arm will fit through the loop *(photo 6 & 7)*.

COW

FINISHED MEASUREMENTS
- ✗ Approx. 7.5 inches tall by 5 inches wide

MATERIALS
- ✗ Worsted weight yarn: white, black, tan, and pink
- ✗ Size G/4.25mm crochet hook
- ✗ Pair of 9mm safety eyes
- ✗ Black embroidery floss and small embroidery needle
- ✗ Polyester fiberfill stuffing
- ✗ Yarn needle
- ✗ Scissors
- ✗ Stitch marker
- ✗ Straight pins (optional, but very helpful when assembling the pieces)

ABBREVIATIONS
- ✗ Mr – Magic ring
- ✗ R – Round
- ✗ Sc – Single crochet
- ✗ Sts – Stitches
- ✗ Inv Dec – Invisible decrease
- ✗ Sl St – Slip stitch
- ✗ Hdc – Half double crochet
- ✗ Dc – Double crochet
- ✗ Tr – Triple crochet

PATTERN NOTES
- ✗ This pattern is crocheted in continuous rounds

HEAD

Using white yarn,

Round 1: 6 sc in magic ring (6 sts)
R2: 2 sc in each st around. (12 sts)
R3: *Sc 1, 2 sc in next st,* 6 times. (18 sts)
R4: *Sc 2, 2 sc in next st,* 6 times. (24 sts)
R5: *Sc 3, 2 sc in next st,* 6 times. (30 sts)
R6: *Sc 4, 2 sc in next st,* 6 times. (36 sts)
R7-12: Sc 36.

Add safety eyes.

R13: *Sc 4, inv dec 1,* 6 times. (30 sts)
R14: *Sc 3, inv dec 1,* 6 times. (24 sts)

Begin stuffing with fiberfill and continue as you go.

R15: *Sc 2, inv dec 1,* 6 times. (18 sts)
R16: *Sc 1, inv dec 1,* 6 times. (12 sts)
R17: Inv dec around 6 times. (6 sts)

Fasten off and close piece.

HORN: MAKE 2

Using tan yarn,

Round 1: 6 sc in magic ring (6 sts)
R2-4: Sc 6.

Fasten off and leave a tail for sewing.

Adding fiberfill is optional as these parts are quite small.

Position horns on the top of the head, about 1 round away from the magic ring *(photos 2 & 3)*.

NOSE

Using pink yarn,

Round 1: 6 sc in magic ring (6 sts)
R2: 2 sc in each st around. (12 sts)
R3-4: Sc 12.

Fasten off and leave a tail for sewing.

For the nose holes — with black embroidery floss and a needle, stitch two lines on both sides of the magic ring.

Stuff with fiberfill and position the nose in between the safety eyes. Sew to head *(photo 1)*.

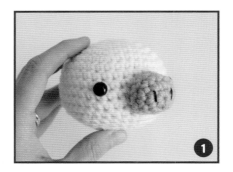

EARS: MAKE 2

Using black yarn,

Round 1: 6 sc in magic ring (6 sts)
R2: Sc 6.
R3: 2 sc in each st around. (12 sts)
R4: *Sc 1, 2 sc in next st,* 6 times. (18 sts)
R5-6: Sc 18.
R7: *Sc 1, inv dec 1,* 6 times. (12 sts)
R8-9: Sc 12.

Fasten off and leave a tail for sewing.

With a yarn needle, weave tail through the sides of ear so that the ear has a "pinched" end (photos 4-7).

Position ears about 3 rounds down from the horns and sew to head. Sew horns and ears to head (photos 8 & 9).

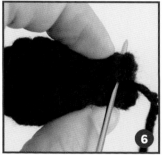

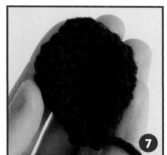

BODY

Using white yarn,

Round 1: 6 sc in magic ring (6 sts)
R2: 2 sc in each st around. (12 sts)
R3: *Sc 1, 2 sc in next st,* 6 times. (18 sts)
R4: *Sc 2, 2 sc in next st,* 6 times. (24 sts)
R5: *Sc 3, 2 sc in next st,* 6 times. (30 sts)
R6-15: Sc 30.
R16: *Sc 3, inv dec 1,* 6 times. (24 sts)

Begin stuffing with fiberfill and continue as you go.

R17: *Sc 2, inv dec 1,* 6 times. (18 sts)
R18: *Sc 1, inv dec 1,* 6 times. (12 sts)
R19: Inv dec around 6 times. (6 sts)

Fasten off and close piece.

TAIL

Using white yarn,

Round 1: 5 sc in magic ring (5 sts)
R2-10: Sc 5.

Fasten off and leave a tail for sewing *(see photo 5 on the following page for reference).*

FEET: MAKE 4

Using tan yarn,

Round 1: 6 sc in magic ring (6 sts)
R2: 2 sc in each st around. (12 sts)
R3: Sc 12 through **BACK** loops only.

Change to white yarn,

R4-9: Sc 12.

Fasten off and leave a tail for sewing.

Position front feet on the body, about 3 stitches apart *(photo 1)*. Position the back feet, leaving about 3 rows in between them and the front feet *(photo 2)*. Place feet about 3 stitches apart *(photo 3)*. Sew feet to body *(photo 4)*.

HAIR FOR TAIL

Using black yarn,

Round 1: 4 sc in magic ring (4 sts)
R2: 2 sc in each st around. (8 sts)
R3: Inv dec around 4 times. (4 sts)

Fasten off and leave a tail for sewing
(photo 5).

Sew hair to the tip of tail *(photo 6)* then
sew the tail to the body *(photo 7)*.

ATTACH HEAD

At this point you'll want to sew the head onto the body. Cut a length of white yarn and position the head on the body. Sew to the body, making sure the head is securely attached *(photos 8 & 9)*.

SPOTS

Using black yarn for all spots.

LARGE SPOT: MAKE 1
Round 1: 7 sc in magic ring (7 sts)
R2: 2 sc in each st around. (14 sts)
R3: In the next round of stitches, do the following: Hdc, hdc dc tr, hdc, dc, dc tr, hdc hdc, dc tr, dc, hdc, hdc, dc, tr, dc, sl st in last stitch.

Fasten off and leave a tail for sewing.

MEDIUM SPOT: MAKE 1
Round 1: 6 sc in magic ring (6 sts)
R2: 2 sc in each st around. (12 sts)
R3: In the next round of stitches, do the following: Sc, hdc sc, sc, sc, hdc dc dc, sc, sc, hdc, dc, sc sc, hdc dc, dc sc, sl st.

Fasten off and leave a tail for sewing.

SMALLER SPOTS

SPOT #1: MAKE 1
Round 1: 7 sc in magic ring (7 sts)
R2: 2 sc in each st around. (14 sts)

Fasten off and leave a tail for sewing.

SPOT #2: MAKE 2
Round 1: 6 sc in magic ring (6 sts)
R2: 2 sc in each st around. (12 sts)

Fasten off and leave a tail for sewing.

SPOT #3: MAKE 1
Round 1: 5 sc in magic ring (5 sts)
R2: 2 sc in each st around. (10 sts)

Fasten off and leave a tail for sewing.

SPOT #4: MAKE 1
Round 1: 6 sc in magic ring (6 sts)

Fasten off and leave a tail for sewing.

SPOTS ASSEMBLY

FOR THE HEAD:
Sew spots #2 (only one), #3 and #4 in various places on the back of the head *(photo 1)*.

FOR THE BODY:
Sew spot #1 and medium spot on the left side of body *(photo 2)*. Sew spot #2 and large spot on the right side of the body *(photo 3)*.

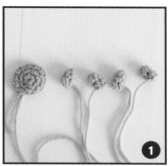

UDDER

MAIN UDDER PIECE: MAKE 1
Using pink yarn,

Round 1: 6 sc in magic ring (6 sts)
R2: 2 sc in each st around. (12 sts)
R3: Sc 12.

Fasten off and leave a tail for sewing.

TEAT: MAKE 4
Using pink yarn,

Round 1: 4 sc in magic ring (4 sts)
R2-3: Sc 4.
Fasten off and leave a tail for sewing.

Sew each teat around the main udder piece *(photos 2 & 3)*. Position the main udder piece in between legs and sew to body *(photo 4)*.

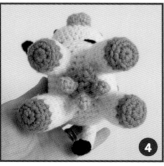

DUCK

- -

FINISHED MEASUREMENTS
- ✂ Approx. 5 inches tall by 5.5 inches wide

MATERIALS
- ✂ Worsted weight yarn: green, gray, yellow, orange, white, blue, and brown
- ✂ Size G/4.25mm crochet hook
- ✂ Pair of 12mm safety eyes
- ✂ Black embroidery floss and small embroidery needle
- ✂ Polyester fiberfill stuffing
- ✂ Yarn needle
- ✂ Scissors
- ✂ Stitch marker
- ✂ Straight pins (optional, but very helpful when assembling the pieces)

ABBREVIATIONS
- ✂ Mr – Magic ring
- ✂ R – Round
- ✂ Sc – Single crochet
- ✂ Sts – Stitches
- ✂ Inv Dec – Invisible decrease
- ✂ Sl St – Slip stitch

PATTERN NOTES
- ✂ This pattern is crocheted in continuous rounds
- ✂ The body contains multiple color changes (Rounds 16–26)
- ✂ To achieve the diagonal lines for the brown section of the body, please reference the clean color changing technique in the Stitches and Techniques section

BODY

Using green yarn,

Round 1: 6 sc in magic ring (6 sts)
R2: 2 sc in each st around. (12 sts)
R3: *Sc 1, 2 sc in next st,* 6 times. (18 sts)
R4: *Sc 2, 2 sc in next st,* 6 times. (24 sts)
R5: *Sc 3, 2 sc in next st,* 6 times. (30 sts)
R6: *Sc 4, 2 sc in next st,* 6 times. (36 sts)
R7: *Sc 5, 2 sc in next st,* 6 times. (42 sts)
R8: *Sc 6, 2 sc in next st,* 6 times. (48 sts)
R9-14: Sc 48.

Change to white yarn,

R15: Sc 48.

Change to gray yarn,

R16: Sc 16 in gray, change to brown yarn *(photos 1-4)* and sc 16, change to gray *(photos 5-8)* and sc 16. (48 sts)

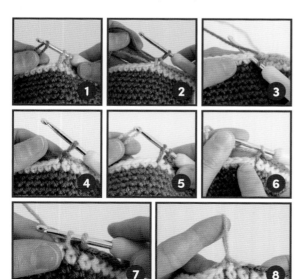

Add safety eyes. Place them in the green section but make sure to place in the middle of the brown stitches *(photo 9)* and leave about 10 stitches in between for the beak.

R17: Sc 16 in gray, sc 17 in brown, sc 15 in gray. (48 sts)
R18: Sc 16 in gray, sc 18 in brown, sc 14 in gray. (48 sts)
R19: Sc 16 in gray, sc 19 in brown, sc 13 in gray. (48 sts)
R20: Sc 16 in gray, sc 20 in brown, sc 12 in gray. (48 sts)
R21: Sc 16 in gray, sc 21 in brown, sc 11 in gray. (48 sts)
R22: Sc 16 in gray, sc 22 in brown, sc 10 in gray. (48 sts)
R23: Sc 16 in gray, sc 23 in brown, sc 9 in gray. (48 sts)
R24: Sc 16 in gray, sc 24 in brown, sc 8 in gray. (48 sts)
R25: Sc 16 in gray, sc 25 in brown, sc 7 in gray. (48 sts)
R26: Sc 16 in gray, sc 26 in brown, sc 6 in gray. (48 sts)
R27: Sc 48 in gray through **BACK** loops only.
R28: *Sc 6, inv dec 1,* 6 times. (42 sts)
R29: *Sc 5, inv dec 1,* 6 times. (36 sts)
R30: *Sc 4, inv dec 1,* 6 times. (30 sts)

Begin to stuff with fiberfill and continue as you go.

R31: *Sc 3, inv dec 1,* 6 times. (24 sts)
R32: *Sc 2, inv dec 1,* 6 times. (18 sts)
R33: *Sc 1, inv dec 1,* 6 times. (12 sts)
R34: Inv dec around 6 times. (6 sts)

Fasten off and close piece.

BEAK

Using yellow yarn,

Round 1: 5 sc in magic ring (5 sts)
R2: 2 sc in each st around. (10 sts)
R3: Sc 10.
R4: *Sc 1, 2 sc in next st,* 5 times. (15 sts)
R5: Sc 15.

Fasten off and leave a tail for sewing.

For the nose holes: with black embroidery floss and a needle, stitch two lines about two stitches apart *(photo 1)*.

Flatten beak then position between the safety eyes and sew to body *(photos 2 & 3)*.

FEET: MAKE 2

Using orange yarn,

Round 1: 6 sc in magic ring (6 sts)
R2: 2 sc in each st around. (12 sts)
R3: *Sc 1, 2 sc in next st,* 6 times. (18 sts)
R4: Sc 18.
R5: *Sc 1, inv dec 1,* 6 times. (12 sts)
R6: *Sc 1, inv dec 1,* 4 times. (8 sts)

Fasten off and leave a tail for sewing.

Flatten feet then position right below **round 27** from body *(photos 4 & 5)*. Sew to body.

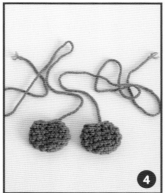

WINGS: MAKE 2

Using gray yarn,

Round 1: 6 sc in magic ring (6 sts)
R2: 2 sc in each st around. (12 sts)
R3: Sc 12.
R4: *Sc 1, 2 sc in next st,* 6 times. (18 sts)
R5-7: Sc 18.
R8: *Sc 1, inv dec 1,* 6 times. (12 sts)
R9-10: Sc 12.
R11: *Sc 1, inv dec 1,* 4 times. (8 sts)
R12: Sc 8.
R13: *Inv dec 1,* 3 times, sc 1. (4 sts)

Fasten off and close piece. With a yarn needle, weave tail through the inside of the wing so that the tail is now near the magic ring *(photos 1 & 2)*. This will be the tail for sewing the wing to the body.

TO ADD THE BLUE LINE:
you will be making a line of 4 X's.

1. First flatten wing. Then with blue yarn and yarn needle *(photo 3)*, insert the needle through the back of the wing and up through rounds 6 and 7 *(photo 4)*. Make sure to bring the needle up through one of the holes near the edge of the wing. Hide the knot on the inside of the wing *(photos 5 & 6)*.

2. Once you have pulled the yarn through, insert the needle into the hole diagonal from the one the needle just came out of (i.e., down and over one stitch, *photos 7 & 8*).

3. Now bring the needle up into the hole above the one the needle just entered. Make an **X** by inserting the needle into the hole diagonal to this corner *(photo 9)*.

4. For the next stitch, bring the needle up through the hole which is diagonal from the final hole for the first **X** *(photo 10)*.

5. Repeat the steps for making an **X** *(photos 11-13)*. The row of **X**'s will be along the bottom of the wing *(photos 14 & 15)*.

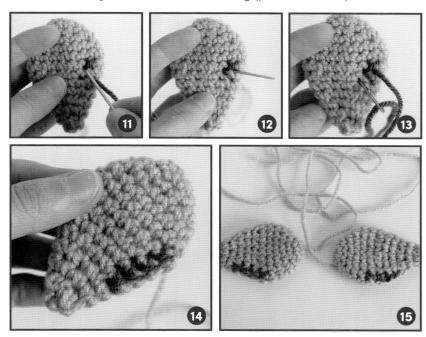

Position the wings near the white line on the body, right where the color changes from gray to brown *(photos 16 & 17)*. Only attach about 5 rows to the body so the wing sticks out just a little *(photo 18)*.

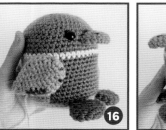

EGGS

FINISHED MEASUREMENTS
- ✕ Large eggs – approx. 2.5 inches tall by 2 inches wide
- ✕ Small eggs – approx. 2 inches tall by 1.5 inches wide

MATERIALS
- ✕ Worsted weight yarn: variety of colors such as white, tan, cream, and blue
- ✕ Size G/4.25mm crochet hook
- ✕ Pair of 9mm safety eyes for each egg
- ✕ Black embroidery floss and small embroidery needle
- ✕ Polyester fiberfill stuffing
- ✕ Yarn needle
- ✕ Scissors
- ✕ Stitch marker
- ✕ Optional – egg carton

ABBREVIATIONS
- ✕ Mr – Magic ring
- ✕ R – Round
- ✕ Sc – Single crochet
- ✕ Sts – Stitches
- ✕ Inv Dec – Invisible decrease

PATTERN NOTES
- ✕ This pattern is crocheted in continuous rounds

LARGE EGG

Using preferred color,

Round 1: 6 sc in magic ring (6 sts)
R2: 2 sc in each st around. (12 sts)
R3: Sc 12.
R4: *Sc 1, 2 sc in next st,* 6 times. (18 sts)
R5: Sc 18.
R6: *Sc 2, 2 sc in next st,* 6 times. (24 sts)
R7-11: Sc 24.

Add safety eyes and stitch mouth.

R12: *Sc 2, inv dec 1,* 6 times. (18 sts)
R13: *Sc 1, inv dec 1,* 6 times. (12 sts)

Add fiberfill stuffing.

R14: Sc 12.
R15: Inv dec around 6 times. (6 sts)

Fasten off and close piece.

SMALL EGG

Using preferred color,

Round 1: 5 sc in magic ring (5 sts)
R2: 2 sc in each st around. (10 sts)
R3: Sc 10.
R4: *Sc 1, 2 sc in next st,* 5 times. (15 sts)
R5: Sc 15.
R6: *Sc 2, 2 sc in next st,* 5 times. (20 sts)
R7-11: Sc 20.

Add safety eyes and stitch mouth.

R12: *Sc 2, inv dec 1,* 5 times. (15 sts)

Add fiberfill stuffing.

R13: *Sc 1, inv dec 1,* 5 times. (10 sts)
R14: Inv dec around 5 times. (5 sts)

Fasten off and close piece.

PIG

FINISHED MEASUREMENTS
- ✕ Approx. 5 inches tall by 4 inches wide

MATERIALS
- ✕ Worsted weight yarn: pink and tan
- ✕ Size G/4.25mm crochet hook
- ✕ Pair of 12mm safety eyes
- ✕ Black embroidery floss and small embroidery needle
- ✕ Polyester fiberfill stuffing
- ✕ Yarn needle
- ✕ Scissors
- ✕ Stitch marker
- ✕ Straight pins (optional, but very helpful when assembling the pieces)

ABBREVIATIONS
- ✕ Mr – Magic ring
- ✕ R – Round
- ✕ Sc – Single crochet
- ✕ Sts – Stitches
- ✕ Inv Dec – Invisible decrease
- ✕ Ch – chain

PATTERN NOTES
- ✕ This pattern is crocheted in continuous rounds

BODY

Using pink yarn,

Round 1: 6 sc in magic ring (6 sts)
R2: 2 sc in each st around. (12 sts)
R3: *Sc 1, 2 sc in next st,* 6 times. (18 sts)
R4: *Sc 2, 2 sc in next st,* 6 times. (24 sts)
R5: *Sc 3, 2 sc in next st,* 6 times. (30 sts)
R6: *Sc 4, 2 sc in next st,* 6 times. (36 sts)
R7: *Sc 5, 2 sc in next st,* 6 times. (42 sts)
R8-24: Sc 42.

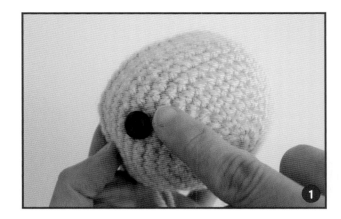

For the eyes - first place the right eye (your left) between rounds 9 and 10 from magic ring (photo 1). For the left eye (your right) count 20 stitches across the top of the pig, over to the right. Place eye in the 21st stitch (photos 2 & 3).

R25: *Sc 5, inv dec 1,* 6 times. (36 sts)

Begin stuffing with fiberfill and continue as you go.

R26: *Sc 4, inv dec 1,* 6 times. (30 sts)
R27: *Sc 3, inv dec 1,* 6 times. (24 sts)
R28: *Sc 2, inv dec 1,* 6 times. (18 sts)
R29: *Sc 1, inv dec 1,* 6 times. (12 sts)
R30: Inv dec around 6 times. (6 sts)

Fasten off and close piece.

SNOUT

Using pink yarn,

Round 1: 5 sc in magic ring (5 sts)
R2: 2 sc in each st around. (10 sts)
R3: *Sc 1, 2 sc in next st,* 5 times. (15 sts)
R4: Sc 15 through **BACK** loops only.
R5-6: Sc 15.

Fasten off and leave a tail for sewing.

For the nose holes – with black embroidery floss and a needle, stitch two lines on both sides of the magic ring *(photo 4)*.

Stuff with fiberfill and position the snout in between the safety eyes *(photo 5)*. Sew to body *(photo 6)*.

EARS: MAKE 2

Using pink yarn,

Round 1: 5 sc in magic ring (5 sts)
R2: Sc 5.
R3: 2 sc in each st around. (10 sts)
R4: *Sc 1, 2 sc in next st,* 5 times. (15 sts)
R5: *Sc 2, 2 sc in next st,* 5 times. (20 sts)
R6: Sc 20.
R7: *Sc 2, inv dec 1,* 5 times. (15 sts)
R8: *Sc 1, inv dec 1,* 5 times. (10 sts)

Fasten off and leave a tail for sewing *(photo 7)*.

Position ears between rounds 13 and 15, spaced about 7 stitches apart *(photos 8 & 9)*. Sew to body.

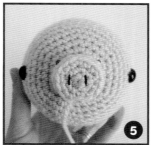
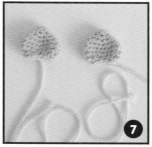

FEET: MAKE 4

Using tan yarn,

Round 1: 6 sc in magic ring (6 sts)
R2: 2 sc in each st around. (12 sts)
R3: Sc 12.
R4: Sc 12 through **BACK** loops only.

Change to pink yarn,

R5-9: Sc 12.

Fasten off and leave a tail for sewing *(photo 10)*.

Stuff with fiberfill. Position front feet by lining them up with the ears *(photo 11)*. Place legs about 4 stitches apart. Position the back feet, leaving about 3-4 rows in between them and the front feet *(photo 12)*. Place back feet about 4 stitches apart. Sew feet to body *(photo 13)*.

TAIL

Using pink yarn,

Ch 9, then in 2nd ch from hook 2 sc in each ch across. (16 total)

Fasten off and leave a tail for sewing. Attach tail to the back of the body and sew in place.

AT THE
BAKERY

COOKIES

FINISHED MEASUREMENTS
- ✕ Approx. 2.5 inches wide

MATERIALS
- ✕ Worsted weight yarn:
  - Chocolate chip – tan and dark brown
  - Frosted sugar cookies – light tan and pink
- ✕ Size G/4.25mm crochet hook
- ✕ 2 pairs of 6mm safety eyes
- ✕ Embroidery floss: black and a few colors for the sprinkles
- ✕ Small embroidery needle
- ✕ Polyester fiberfill stuffing
- ✕ Yarn needle
- ✕ Scissors
- ✕ Stitch marker

ABBREVIATIONS
- ✕ Mr – Magic ring
- ✕ R – Round
- ✕ Sc – Single crochet
- ✕ Inv Dec – Invisible decrease
- ✕ Sts – Stitches

PATTERN NOTES
- ✕ This pattern is crocheted in continuous rounds
- ✕ Pattern is assembled as you go

CHOCOLATE CHIP COOKIE

Using tan yarn,

Round 1: 6 sc in magic ring (6 sts)
R2: 2 sc in each st around. (12 sts)
R3: *Sc 1, 2 sc in next st,* 6 times. (18 sts)
R4: *Sc 2, 2 sc in next st,* 6 times. (24 sts)
R5: *Sc 3, 2 sc in next st,* 6 times. (30 sts)
R6: *Sc 4, 2 sc in next st,* 6 times. (36 sts)
R7–8: Sc 36.
R9: *Sc 4, inv dec 1,* 6 times, through **BACK** loops only. (30 sts)

Add safety eyes and stitch mouth *(photo 1)*.

R10: *Sc 3, inv dec 1,* 6 times. (24 sts)
R11: *Sc 2, inv dec 1,* 6 times. (18 sts)
R12: *Sc 1, inv dec 1,* 6 times. (12 sts)

Add a little bit of fiberfill stuffing.

R13: Inv dec around 6 times. (6 sts)
Fasten off and close piece.

FOR CHOCOLATE CHIPS: with dark brown yarn, stitch lines in various places all over the cookie *(photo 2)*.

FROSTED SUGAR COOKIE

FROSTING:

Using pink yarn,

Round 1: 6 sc in magic ring (6 sts)
R2: 2 sc in each st around. (12 sts)
R3: *Sc 1, 2 sc in next st,* 6 times. (18 sts)
R4: *Sc 2, 2 sc in next st,* 6 times. (24 sts)
R5: *Sc 3, 2 sc in next st,* 6 times. (30 sts)
R6: Sc 30.

Fasten off and leave a tail for sewing.

Set aside.

SUGAR COOKIE:

Using light tan yarn,

Round 1: 6 sc in magic ring (6 sts)
R2: 2 sc in each st around. (12 sts)
R3: *Sc 1, 2 sc in next st,* 6 times. (18 sts)
R4: *Sc 2, 2 sc in next st,* 6 times. (24 sts)
R5: *Sc 3, 2 sc in next st,* 6 times. (30 sts)
R6: *Sc 4, 2 sc in next st,* 6 times. (36 sts)
R7: Sc 36.
R8: *Sc 4, inv dec 1,* 6 times, through **BACK** loops only. (30 sts)

Sew frosting to cookie base *(photo 1)*.

Add safety eyes, push through both frosting and cookie *(photos 2 & 3)* and then add safety backings.

Stitch mouth and sprinkles *(photos 4 & 5)*.

R9: *Sc 3, inv dec 1,* 6 times. (24 sts)
R10: *Sc 2, inv dec 1,* 6 times. (18 sts)
R11: *Sc 1, inv dec 1,* 6 times. (12 sts)

Add a little bit of fiberfill stuffing *(photos 6 & 7)*.

R12: Inv dec around 6 times. (6 sts)

Fasten off and close piece.

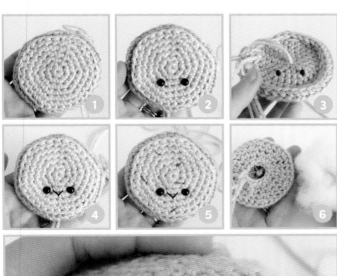

CUPCAKES

FINISHED MEASUREMENTS
- ✗ Jumbo — Approx. 4.5 inches wide by 4.5 inches tall
- ✗ Regular — Approx. 3.5 inches wide by 3.5 inches tall

MATERIALS
- ✗ Worsted weight yarn: tan, and any color for the frosting
- ✗ Size G/4.25mm crochet hook
- ✗ Pair of 9mm safety eyes
- ✗ Embroidery floss: black, and a few colors for the sprinkles
- ✗ Small embroidery needle
- ✗ Polyester fiberfill stuffing
- ✗ Yarn needle
- ✗ Scissors
- ✗ Stitch marker
- ✗ Cardboard – for jumbo cupcake only
- ✗ Optional:
  - Cheeks – pink felt or pink embroidery floss and size E crochet hook

ABBREVIATIONS
- ✗ Mr – Magic ring
- ✗ R – Round
- ✗ Sc – Single crochet
- ✗ Sts – Stitches
- ✗ Inv Dec – Invisible decrease
- ✗ Sl St – Slip stitch
- ✗ Hdc – Half double crochet
- ✗ Sk – skip

PATTERN NOTES
- ✗ This pattern is crocheted in continuous rounds
- ✗ Cupcakes use the same technique for assembly
- ✗ Optional - add a piece of cardboard to jumbo cupcake for a more solid base

REGULAR CUPCAKE

CAKE:

Using tan yarn,

Round 1: 6 sc in magic ring (6 sts)
R2: 2 sc in each st around. (12 sts)
R3: *Sc 1, 2 sc in next st,* 6 times. (18 sts)
R4: *Sc 2, 2 sc in next st,* 6 times. (24 sts)
R5: *Sc 3, 2 sc in next st,* 6 times. (30 sts)
R6: *Sc 4, 2 sc in next st,* 6 times. (36 sts)
R7: *Sc 4, inv dec 1,* 6 times through **BACK** loops only. (30 sts)
R8: *Sc 4, 2 sc in next st,* 6 times. (36 sts)
R9-13: Sc 36.

Fasten off and leave a long tail for sewing.

Add safety eyes and stitch mouth.

Set aside.

FROSTING:

Using pink yarn,

Round 1: 6 sc in magic ring (6 sts)
R2: 2 sc in each st around. (12 sts)
R3: *Sc 1, 2 sc in next st,* 6 times. (18 sts)
R4: *Sc 2, 2 sc in next st,* 6 times. (24 sts)
R5: *Sc 3, 2 sc in next st,* 6 times. (30 sts)
R6: *Sc 4, 2 sc in next st,* 6 times. (36 sts)
R7: *Sc 5, 2 sc in next st,* 6 times. (42 sts)
R8-12: Sc 42.
R13: *Sc 5, inv dec 1,* 6 times. (36 sts)
R14: *4 hdc, sk 1 st, sl st in next st,* 12 times through **FRONT** loops only. (60 sts)

Fasten off and weave in end.

With embroidery floss, sew sprinkles in various places.

OPTIONAL:
Felt cheeks – cut two small circles of pink felt and sew near safety eyes.

OR

Crochet cheeks – with pink embroidery floss and Size E hook,

Round 1: 7 sc in magic ring.

Fasten off. Sew near safety eyes.

JUMBO CUPCAKE

CAKE:
Using tan yarn,

Round 1: 6 sc in magic ring (6 sts)
R2: 2 sc in each st around. (12 sts)
R3: *Sc 1, 2 sc in next st,* 6 times. (18 sts)
R4: *Sc 2, 2 sc in next st,* 6 times. (24 sts)
R5: *Sc 3, 2 sc in next st,* 6 times. (30 sts)
R6: *Sc 4, 2 sc in next st,* 6 times. (36 sts)
R7: *Sc 5, 2 sc in next st,* 6 times. (42 sts)
R8: *Sc 6, 2 sc in next st,* 6 times. (48 sts)
R9: *Sc 6, inv dec 1,* 6 times through **BACK** loops only. (42 sts)
R10: Sc 6, 2 sc in next st,* 6 times. (48 sts)
R11-19: Sc 48.

Fasten off and leave a long tail for sewing.

Add safety eyes and stitch mouth.

Follow directions from Stitches and Techniques on page 20 to add in eyelashes! Set aside.

FROSTING:
Using pink yarn,

Round 1: 6 sc in magic ring (6 sts)
R2: 2 sc in each st around. (12 sts)
R3: *Sc 1, 2 sc in next st,* 6 times. (18 sts)
R4: *Sc 2, 2 sc in next st,* 6 times. (24 sts)
R5: *Sc 3, 2 sc in next st,* 6 times. (30 sts)
R6: *Sc 4, 2 sc in next st,* 6 times. (36 sts)
R7: *Sc 5, 2 sc in next st,* 6 times. (42 sts)
R8: *Sc 6, 2 sc in next st,* 6 times. (48 sts)
R9: *Sc 7, 2 sc in next st,* 6 times. (54 sts)
R10-15: Sc 54.
R16: *Sc 7, inv dec 1,* 6 times. (48 sts)
R17: *5 hdc, sk 1 st, sl st in next st,* 16 times through **FRONT** loops only. (96 sts)

Fasten off and weave in end.

With embroidery floss, sew sprinkles in various places.

OPTIONAL:

Felt cheeks - cut two small circles of pink felt and sew near safety eyes.

OR

Crochet cheeks - with pink embroidery floss and Size E hook,

Round 1: 9 sc in magic ring.

Fasten off. Sew near safety eyes.

ASSEMBLY

1. For jumbo cupcake - trace base of cake on a piece of cardboard and insert before sewing pieces together *(photo 1)*.

2. With tail from cake and a yarn needle, begin to weave needle through the back loops of **R17** from frosting and **R19** from cake *(photos 2 & 3)*. By weaving through these stitches, it will create a clean finish and your stitching will be hidden *(photos 4-6)*.

3. Add fiberfill stuffing before closing piece. Secure with a knot and hide inside the cupcake.

MACARONS

FINISHED MEASUREMENTS
- Approx. 2 inches wide by 1.5 inches tall

MATERIALS
- Worsted weight yarn: pick two colors, one for the cookie and one for the filling
- Size G/4.25mm crochet hook
- Pair of 6mm safety eyes
- Black embroidery floss and small embroidery needle
- Polyester fiberfill stuffing
- Yarn needle
- Scissors
- Stitch marker

ABBREVIATIONS
- Mr – Magic ring
- R – Round
- Sc – Single crochet
- Sts – Stitches
- Sl St – Slip stitch

PATTERN NOTES
- This pattern is crocheted in continuous rounds

MACARON

TOP PIECE:
Using green yarn,

Round 1: 6 sc in magic ring (6 sts)
R2: 2 sc in each st around. (12 sts)
R3: *Sc 1, 2 sc in next st,* 6 times. (18 sts)
R4: *Sc 2, 2 sc in next st,* 6 times. (24 sts)
R5: *Sc 3, 2 sc in next st,* 6 times. (30 sts)
R6: Sl st in each st around. (30 sts) *(photo 1)*

Change to light green *(photo 2)*,

The next round will be done in the row of stitches
BEHIND the slip stitches from **R6** *(photo 3)*.

R7: Sl st in each st around. (30 sts) *(photo 4)*
R8: Sc 30. *(photo 5)*

Fasten off and leave a tail for sewing.

BOTTOM PIECE:
Using green yarn,

Round 1: 6 sc in magic ring (6 sts)
R2: 2 sc in each st around. (12 sts)
R3: *Sc 1, 2 sc in next st,* 6 times. (18 sts)
R4: *Sc 2, 2 sc in next st,* 6 times. (24 sts)
R5: *Sc 3, 2 sc in next st,* 6 times. (30 sts)
R6: Sl st in each st around. (30 sts)

Fasten off and weave in tail.

ASSEMBLY

With a yarn needle, begin sewing the two pieces together. To achieve a smooth finish, weave needle through the stitches of **R8** from the top piece and the row of stitches behind the slip stitches from **R6** on the bottom piece *(photos 2-4)*. Be sure to add fiberfill stuffing before closing the piece *(photo 6)*.

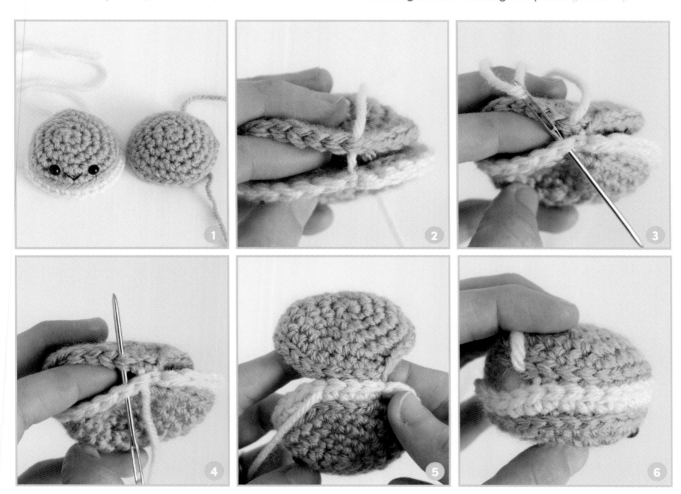

MUG & DONUT

FINISHED MEASUREMENTS
- ✕ Mug – approx. 2.5 inches tall by 2.5 inches wide
- ✕ Donut – approx. 4 inches tall by 1.5 inches tall

MATERIALS
- ✕ Worsted weight yarn: choose any color for the mug and donut frosting
  - • For the mug: brown, and choose any color for the mug (pattern uses blue)
  - • For the donut: tan, and choose any color for the frosting
- ✕ Size G/4.25mm crochet hook
- ✕ Pair of 9mm safety eyes
- ✕ Embroidery floss: black and choose any colors for sprinkles
- ✕ Small embroidery needle
- ✕ Polyester fiberfill stuffing
- ✕ Yarn needle
- ✕ Scissors
- ✕ Stitch marker
- ✕ Optional:
  - • Cheeks – pink felt or pink embroidery floss and size E crochet hook

ABBREVIATIONS
- ✕ Mr – Magic ring
- ✕ Ch – Chain
- ✕ R – Round
- ✕ Sc – Single crochet
- ✕ Dc – Double crochet
- ✕ Sts – Stitches
- ✕ Inv Dec – Invisible decrease
- ✕ Sl St – Slip stitch
- ✕ Hdc – Half double crochet
- ✕ Tr – Triple crochet

PATTERN NOTES
- ✕ Mug pattern is crocheted in continuous rounds and is assembled as you go
- ✕ Donut and frosting pieces start as a chain then are connected to form a ring
  Each piece is then crocheted in continuous rounds

MUG

HANDLE:
Leave tail at beginning for sewing.

Using blue yarn, Ch 17.
Row 1: In 2nd ch from hook hdc in each ch across. (16 total)

Fasten off and leave another tail for sewing.

Set aside *(photo 1)*.

CUP:
Using blue yarn,

Round 1: 6 sc in magic ring (6 sts)
R2: 2 sc in each st around. (12 sts)
R3: *Sc 1, 2 sc in next st,* 6 times. (18 sts)
R4: *Sc 2, 2 sc in next st,* 6 times. (24 sts)
R5: *Sc 3, 2 sc in next st,* 6 times. (30 sts)
R6: *Sc 4, 2 sc in next st,* 6 times. (36 sts)
R7: Sc 36 through **BACK** loops only.
R8–18: Sc 36.

Fasten off and weave in tail *(photo 2)*.

ATTACH THE HANDLE:
Starting with the tail from the handle, sew bottom part of the handle to the cup *(right above the rim, photos 3 & 4)*. Secure with a knot and cut tail. With the finishing tail, insert into bottom of cup and weave to the top. Fold top of handle over about ½ inch *(photo 5)* and use finishing tail to sew handle to cup *(photos 6 & 7)*. Secure with a knot and cut tail.

Add safety eyes and stitch mouth *(photo 8)*.

COFFEE PIECE:
Using brown yarn,

Round 1: 6 sc in magic ring (6 sts)
R2: 2 sc in each st around. (12 sts)
R3: *Sc 1, 2 sc in next st,* 6 times. (18 sts)
R4: *Sc 2, 2 sc in next st,* 6 times. (24 sts)
R5: *Sc 3, 2 sc in next st,* 6 times. (30 sts)
R6: *Sc 4, 2 sc in next st,* 6 times. (36 sts)

Fasten off and leave a tail for sewing.

Sew coffee piece to mug. Weave yarn needle through the horizontal stitches (photos 9–12), just below **R18** from mug. Add fiberfill stuffing to mug before closing up hole.

123

DONUT

CAKE:
*Make sure before Round 1 that the chain is **NOT** twisted.*

Using tan yarn,

Ch 21, then sl st into the 1st ch to form a circle. Ch 1. *(photos 1 & 2)*

 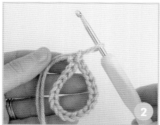

Round 1: *Sc 2, 2 sc in next st,* 7 times. (28 sts)
R2: *Sc 3, 2 sc in next st,* 7 times. (35 sts)
R3: *Sc 4, 2 sc in next st,* 7 times. (42 sts)
R4: *Sc 5, 2 sc in next st,* 7 times. (49 sts)
R5-8: Sc 49.
R9: *Sc 5, inv dec 1,* 7 times. (42 sts)
R10: *Sc 4, inv dec 1,* 7 times. (35 sts)
R11: *Sc 3, inv dec 1,* 7 times. (28 sts)
R12: *Sc 2, inv dec 1,* 7 times. (21 sts)

Fasten off and leave a long tail for sewing.

Add safety eyes and stitch mouth *(photo 3)*.

To sew up donut hole, flatten so that both openings are together. Weave yarn needle back and forth through the stitches on the edge *(photo 4-7)*. Make sure to add fiberfill stuffing as you sew the donut hole.

FROSTING:

Leave a tail at the beginning for sewing! Before Round 1, make sure that the chain is **NOT** twisted.

Using white yarn,

Ch 21, then sl st into the 1st ch to form a circle. Ch 1. *(photos 8 & 9)*

Round 1: *Sc 2, 2 sc in next st,* 7 times. (28 sts)
R2: *Sc 3, 2 sc in next st,* 7 times. (35 sts)
R3: *Sc 4, 2 sc in next st,* 7 times. (42 sts)
R4: *Sc 5, 2 sc in next st,* 7 times. (49 sts)

To make the icing drips along the rim *(photos 12 & 13)*, crochet the following stitches in the next round,

R5: *Sc 3, hdc & dc in next st, 2 tr in next st, dc & hdc in next st*,
    Sc 5, hdc & dc in next st, dc & hdc in next st,
    Sc 5, hdc & dc in next st, 2 tr in next st, dc & hdc in next st,
    Sc 5, hdc & dc in next st, dc & hdc in next st,
    Sc 5, hdc & dc in next st, 2 tr in next st, dc & hdc in next st,
    Sc 5, hdc & dc in next st, dc & hdc in next st,
    Sc 6. (64 sts at the end)

Fasten off and leave another tail for sewing. With embroidery floss, sew sprinkles in various places *(photo 14)*.

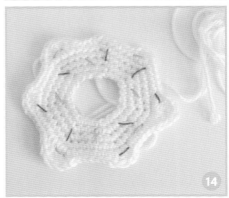

ASSEMBLY

1. With the tail from the beginning of frosting, sew the center of frosting around the middle of the donut *(photos 1-3)*. Secure with a knot and hide end inside donut.

 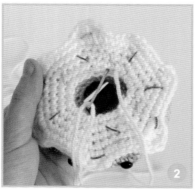 

2. With the tail from the end of the frosting, weave the yarn needle through the last row of stitches (the icing drips) and the donut *(photo 4-6)*. Secure with a knot and hide end inside donut.

PIE

FINISHED MEASUREMENTS

✕ Approx. 1.5 inches tall by 3 inches wide

MATERIALS

✕ Worsted weight yarn: tan for crust, any color for pie filling (pattern uses orange), white
✕ Size G/4.25mm crochet hook
✕ Pair of 9mm safety eyes
✕ Black embroidery floss and small embroidery needle
✕ Polyester fiberfill stuffing
✕ Yarn needle
✕ Scissors
✕ Stitch marker
✕ Optional:
  • Cheeks – pink felt or pink embroidery floss and Size E crochet hook
  • Cardboard – to make the sides of pie more flat
  • Cherry – red and green yarn plus a pair of 6mm eyes

ABBREVIATIONS

✕ Ch – Chain
✕ R – Row
✕ Sc – Single crochet
✕ Sts – Stitches
✕ Hdc – Half double crochet
✕ Dc – Double crochet
✕ Sl St – Slip stitch
✕ Mr – Magic ring
✕ Rnd – Round
✕ Inv dec – Invisible decrease

PATTERN NOTES

✕ Pieces are crocheted flat, then sewn together
✕ Cardboard is added at the end right before closing piece and adding fiberfill
✕ Top and bottom crust pieces are crocheted the same way, with the exception of the bottom piece which has R18–25

PIE CRUST

TOP PIECE:
The color of the pie can vary. For a pie with a top crust, crochet piece in crust color.
Or if making a pie with no top crust, crochet the piece using the filling color.

Using orange yarn, Ch 2.

Row 1: In 2nd ch from hook, sc 2. (2 sts) Ch 1 and turn.
R2: 2 sc in each sc across. (4 sts) Ch 1 and turn.
R3: Sc 4. Ch 1 and turn.
R4: 2 sc in 1st sc, sc 2, 2 sc in last sc. (6 sts) Ch 1 and turn.
R5-6: Sc 6. Ch 1 and turn.
R7: 2 sc in 1st sc, sc 4, 2 sc in last sc. (8 sts) Ch 1 and turn.
R8-9: Sc 8. Ch 1 and turn.
R10: 2 sc in 1st sc, sc 6, 2 sc in last sc. (10 sts) Ch 1 and turn.
R11-12: Sc 10. Ch 1 and turn.
R13: 2 sc in 1st sc, sc 8, 2 sc in last sc. (12 sts) Ch 1 and turn.
R14-15: Sc 12. Ch 1 and turn.
R16: 2 sc in 1st sc, sc 10, 2 sc in last sc. (14 sts) Ch 1 and turn.
R17: Sc 14.

Fasten off and leave a tail for sewing.

BOTTOM PIECE:
Using tan yarn, Ch 2.

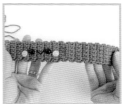

Row 1: In 2nd ch from hook, sc 2. (2 sts) Ch 1 and turn.
R2: 2 sc in each sc across. (4 sts) Ch 1 and turn.
R3: Sc 4. Ch 1 and turn.
R4: 2 sc in 1st sc, sc 2, 2 sc in last sc. (6 sts) Ch 1 and turn.
R5-6: Sc 6. Ch 1 and turn.
R7: 2 sc in 1st sc, sc 4, 2 sc in last sc. (8 sts) Ch 1 and turn.
R8-9: Sc 8. Ch 1 and turn.
R10: 2 sc in 1st sc, sc 6, 2 sc in last sc. (10 sts) Ch 1 and turn.
R11-12: Sc 10. Ch 1 and turn.
R13: 2 sc in 1st sc, sc 8, 2 sc in last sc. (12 sts) Ch 1 and turn.
R14-15: Sc 12. Ch 1 and turn.
R16: 2 sc in 1st sc, sc 10, 2 sc in last sc. (14 sts) Ch 1 and turn.
R17-18: Sc 14. Ch 1 and turn.
R19: Sc 14 through **FRONT** loops only. Ch 1 and turn.
R20-24: Sc 14. Ch 1 and turn.
R25: *hdc dc hdc in first st, sl st in next st, sc 1 in next st,* 5 times.

Fasten off and leave a tail for sewing.

Sides:
Using orange yarn, Ch 6.

Row 1: In 2nd ch from hook, sc 5 across. (5 sts) Ch 1 and turn.
R2-17: Sc 5. Ch 1 and turn.
R18: Sc 5 through **FRONT** loops only. Ch 1 and turn.
R19-34: Sc 5. Ch 1 and turn.

Fasten off and leave a tail for sewing.

Add safety eyes and stitch mouth.

OPTIONAL:

Felt cheeks – cut two small circles of pink felt and sew near safety eyes.

OR

Crochet cheeks – with pink embroidery floss and Size E hook, **Round 1:** 5 sc in magic ring.

Fasten off. Sew near safety eyes.

WHIPPED CREAM

Using white yarn, Ch 39.

Row 1: In 2nd ch from hook, sc in each ch across. (38 sts)

Fasten off and leave a tail for sewing.

To form the little dollop of whipped cream, begin by taking the end with no tails and rolling it together *(photo 2)*. Continue to wrap around until you have formed a circle *(photo 3)*. With a yarn needle, weave one tail through the whipped cream and make sure all sides have been sewn together *(photos 4 & 5)*. You don't want any parts of the chain to come unravelled. Leave tails for attaching to pie at the end.

ASSEMBLY

1. If adding cardboard - trace top piece of pie onto cardboard and cut out. Do the same for the bottom, leaving off the "back" crust (**R19-25** from bottom piece pattern) Set aside *(photo 1 & 2)*.

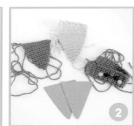

2. Sew the side piece to the bottom crust piece, starting with the shorter side *(photo 3)*. Next sew side to the bottom of the crust and continue sewing until you have reached the other side *(photos 4 & 5)*. Sew the shorter side to the bottom crust as well.

3. Sew the top piece to the **SIDES** only *(photos 6 & 7)*. Leave an opening between the back piece and add cardboard and fiberfill.

4. With the tail from crust, begin to sew the opening closed. Weave the yarn needle through the horizontal stitches behind the last row of the top piece *(these stitches are on the inside of the top piece, photo 8)*. Bring the needle through the first row of horizontal lines on the crust, right below the "scalloped" part of crust *(photos 9 & 10)*.

5. To attach the dollop of whipped cream – take one tail and a yarn needle and begin to sew through the bottom of whipped cream and top of pie *(photos 11 & 12)*. Continue until it is completely attached. Weave in the extra tail and secure with a knot. To "fluff" whipped cream, gently pull on the pieces *(photos 13 & 14)*.

BONUS! MINI CHERRY FOR CHERRY PIE

CHERRY:
Using red yarn,

Round 1: 4 sc in magic ring (4 sts)
Rnd2: 2 sc in each st around. (8 sts)
Rnd3: *Sc 1, 2 sc in next st,* 4 times. (12 sts)
Rnd4-6: Sc 12.

Add safety eyes and stitch mouth.

Add fiberfill stuffing.

Rnd7: *Sc 1, inv dec 1,* 4 times. (8 sts)
Rnd8: Inv dec around 4 times. (4 sts)

Fasten off and close piece.

STEM:
Using green yarn, Ch 8.

Row 1: In 2nd ch from hook, sl st in each ch across. (7 sts)

Fasten off and leave a tail for sewing.

Sew stem to top of cherry.

AT THE MARKET

BELL PEPPER

FINISHED MEASUREMENTS
- ✕ Approx. 4.5 inches tall by 3.5 inches wide

MATERIALS
- ✕ Worsted weight yarn: green and light green
- ✕ Size G/4.25mm crochet hook
- ✕ Pair of 9mm safety eyes
- ✕ Black embroidery floss and small embroidery needle
- ✕ Polyester fiberfill stuffing
- ✕ Yarn needle
- ✕ Scissors
- ✕ Stitch marker
- ✕ Straight pins (optional, but very helpful when assembling the top piece)

ABBREVIATIONS
- ✕ Mr – Magic ring
- ✕ R – Round
- ✕ Sts – Stitches
- ✕ Inv Dec – Invisible decrease
- ✕ Sc – Single crochet

PATTERN NOTES
- ✕ This pattern is crocheted in continuous rounds

BELL PEPPER

Using green yarn,

Round 1: 6 sc in magic ring (6 sts)
R2: 2 sc in each st around. (12 sts)
R3: *Sc 1, 2 sc in next st,* 6 times. (18 sts)
R4: *Sc 2, 2 sc in next st,* 6 times. (24 sts)
R5: *Sc 3, 2 sc in next st,* 6 times. (30 sts)
R6: *Sc 4, 2 sc in next st,* 6 times. (36 sts)
R7: *Sc 5, 2 sc in next st,* 6 times. (42 sts)
R8: *Sc 6, 2 sc in next st,* 6 times. (48 sts)
R9–11: Sc 48.
R12: *Sc 6, inv dec 1,* 6 times. (42 sts)
R13: Sc 42.
R14: *Sc 5, inv dec 1,* 6 times. (36 sts)
R15–20: Sc 36.

Add safety eyes and stitch mouth.

R21: *Sc 4, inv dec 1,* 6 times. (30 sts)
R22: Sc 30.

Begin adding fiberfill and continue as you go.

R23: *Sc 3, inv dec 1,* 6 times. (24 sts)
R24: *Sc 2, inv dec 1,* 6 times. (18 sts)
R25: *Sc 1, inv dec 1,* 6 times. (12 sts)
R26: Inv dec around 6 times. (6 sts)

Fasten off and close piece, leaving a long tail for making indents.

TO MAKE THE INDENTS:

1. With the long tail and a yarn needle, insert needle in the middle of R26 (photo 1). Weave needle up through to the middle of the top magic ring (R1, photo 2). Pull gently.

2. Bring yarn down on one side (photo 3) and insert needle back into the middle of R26 (photo 4). Weave needle up to the top magic ring again (photo 5). Bring yarn down on one side again to make another section (photo 6). Repeat steps until you have made 4 sections total (photo 7).

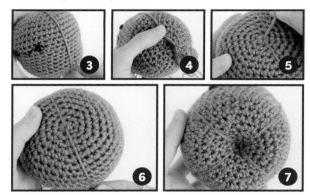

3. The tail will end at the top of the bell pepper (photo 8). Tie a knot and trim tail.

STEM

Using light green yarn,

Round 1: 4 sc in magic ring (4 sts)
R2: 2 sc in each st around. (8 sts)
R3: Sc 8 through **BACK** loops only.
R4-6: Sc 8.
R7: *Sc 1, 2 sc in next st,* 4 times. (12 sts)
R8: *Sc 2, 2 sc in next st,* 4 times. (16 sts)
R9: *Sc 3, 2 sc in next st,* 4 times. (20 sts)

Fasten off and leave a tail for sewing.

Add fiberfill to stem.

Position stem on top of bell pepper. With yarn needle, sew stem to the bell pepper *(photos 2 & 3)*.

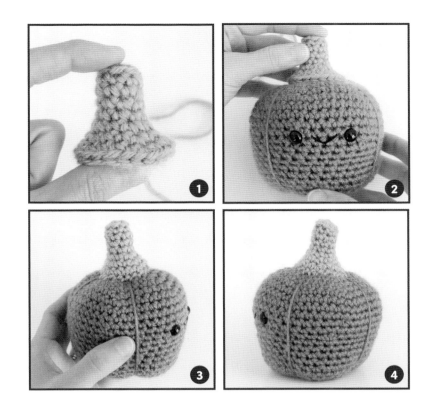

BERRIES

FINISHED MEASUREMENTS
- ✕ Blueberry – Approx. 2.5 inches tall by 2.5 inches wide
- ✕ Strawberry – Approx. 2.5 inches tall by 2.5 inches wide

MATERIALS
- ✕ Worsted weight yarn:
  - Blueberry – blue
  - Strawberry – red and green
- ✕ Size G/4.25mm crochet hook
- ✕ Pair of 9mm safety eyes for each fruit
- ✕ Black and white embroidery floss
- ✕ Small embroidery needle
- ✕ Polyester fiberfill stuffing
- ✕ Yarn needle
- ✕ Scissors
- ✕ Stitch marker
- ✕ Optional – berry basket
- ✕

ABBREVIATIONS
- ✕ Mr – Magic ring
- ✕ R – Round
- ✕ Sc – Single crochet
- ✕ Sts – Stitches
- ✕ Inv Dec – Invisible decrease
- ✕ Sl St – Slip stitch
- ✕ Dc – Double crochet
- ✕ Ch – Chain

PATTERN NOTES
- ✕ This pattern is crocheted in continuous rounds

BLUEBERRY

Using blue yarn,

Round 1: 6 sc in magic ring (6 sts)
R2: 2 sc in each st around. (12 sts)
R3: *Sc 1, 2 sc in next st,* 6 times. (18 sts)
R4: *Sc 2, 2 sc in next st,* 6 times. (24 sts)
R5: *Sc 3, 2 sc in next st,* 6 times. (30 sts)
R6–10: Sc 30.

Add safety eyes and stitch mouth.

R11: *Sc 3, inv dec 1,* 6 times. (24 sts)
R12: *Sc 2, inv dec 1,* 6 times. (18 sts)

Stuff with fiberfill, and continue as you go.

R13: *Sc 1, inv dec 1,* 6 times. (12 sts)
R14: Inv dec around 6 times. (6 sts)

Fasten off and close piece.

BLUEBERRY TOP

Leave a tail at the beginning.

Using blue yarn,

Ch 18, then in 2nd ch from hook *dc in one st, then sl st in next st,* 9 times.

Fasten off and leave a tail for sewing *(photo 1)*.

TO ATTACH TOP TO BLUEBERRY:

1. Bring ends of top together to form a circle *(photo 2)*. With the ending tail and yarn needle, sew ends together *(photos 3 & 4)*. Don't secure with a knot.

2. Position blueberry top around the magic ring on the top of the blueberry.

3. Now with the starting tail and yarn needle, weave starting tail through the stitches on the blueberry and secure with a knot *(photos 5 & 6)*. Trim tail and hide yarn inside the blueberry.

4. Pick up the ending tail again *(photo 7)* and use this piece of yarn to sew the top piece to the blueberry *(photos 8 & 9)*. Secure with knot and hide yarn inside the blueberry.

STRAWBERRY

Using red yarn,

Round 1: 6 sc in magic ring (6 sts)
R2: Sc 6.
R3: 2 sc in each st around. (12 sts)
R4: Sc 12.
R5: *Sc 1, 2 sc in next st,* 6 times. (18 sts)
R6–7: Sc 18.
R8: *Sc 2, 2 sc in next st,* 6 times. (24 sts)
R9: Sc 24.
R10: *Sc 3, 2 sc in next st,* 6 times. (30 sts)
R11: *Sc 3, inv dec 1,* 6 times. (24 sts)

Add safety eyes and stitch mouth.

Stitch seeds in various places with white embroidery floss.*

R12: *Sc 2, inv dec 1,* 6 times. (18 sts)

Begin stuffing with fiberfill and continue as you go.

R13: *Sc 1, inv dec 1,* 6 times. (12 sts)
R14: Inv dec around 6 times. (6 sts)

Fasten off and close piece.

*For the seeds, start at the bottom tip and work up *(photos 1–3)*. Leave needle and white thread and complete R12 *(photo 4)*. Stitch more seeds before closing strawberry piece *(photo 5)*.

LEAF

Using green yarn,

Round 1: 8 sc in magic ring (8 sts)
R2: 2 sc in each st around. (16 sts)
R3: *Sc 1, ch 5, then in 2nd ch from hook sc 1 in each ch across (4 sc total), sl st into original sc, sc 1 into the next st,* 8 times (8 leaves total) *(photos 1–6)*.

Fasten off and leave a tail for sewing.

Position piece on top of strawberry *(photo 7)*. Insert the needle into both the leaf and strawberry, bringing the needle back up to the leaf piece *(photos 8 & 9)*. With a yarn needle, weave it between **R2** and **R3**. The stitching will form a horizontal line of stitches between **R2** and **R3** *(photos 10–12)*. Secure with a knot and hide yarn inside the strawberry.

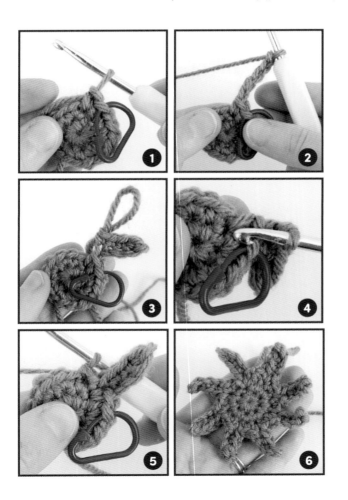

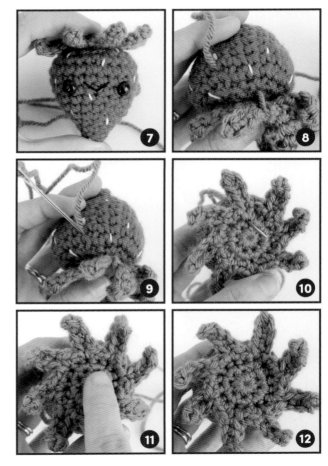

FINISHED MEASUREMENTS
- ✗ Approx. 6.5 inches tall by 3 inches wide

MATERIALS
- ✗ Worsted weight yarn: purple and green
- ✗ Size G/4.25mm crochet hook
- ✗ Pair of 9mm safety eyes for each fruit
- ✗ Black embroidery floss and small embroidery needle
- ✗ Polyester fiberfill stuffing
- ✗ Yarn needle
- ✗ Scissors
- ✗ Stitch marker
- ✗ Straight pins (optional, but very helpful when assembling the top piece)

ABBREVIATIONS
- ✗ Mr – Magic ring
- ✗ R – Round
- ✗ Sc – Single crochet
- ✗ Sts – Stitches
- ✗ Inv Dec – Invisible decrease
- ✗ Ch – Chain
- ✗ Hdc – Half double crochet
- ✗ Dc – Double crochet
- ✗ Tr – Triple crochet
- ✗ Sl St – Slip stitch
- ✗ Sk – Skip

PATTERN NOTES
- ✗ This pattern is crocheted in continuous rounds

EGGPLANT

Using purple yarn,

Round 1: 6 sc in magic ring (6 sts)
R2: 2 sc in each st around. (12 sts)
R3: *Sc 1, 2 sc in next st,* 6 times. (18 sts)
R4: *Sc 2, 2 sc in next st,* 6 times. (24 sts)
R5-7: Sc 24.
R8: *Sc 3, 2 sc in next st,* 6 times. (30 sts)
R9-14: Sc 30.
R15: *Sc 4, 2 sc in next st,* 6 times. (36 sts)
R16-19: Sc 36.
R20: *Sc 5, 2 sc in next st,* 6 times. (42 sts)
R21-23: Sc 42.
R24: *Sc 5, inv dec 1,* 6 times. (36 sts)
R25: *Sc 4, inv dec 1,* 6 times. (30 sts)

Add safety eyes and stitch mouth.

R26: Sc 30.

Begin stuffing with fiberfill and continue as you go.

R27: *Sc 3, inv dec 1,* 6 times. (24 sts)
R28: *Sc 2, inv dec 1,* 6 times. (18 sts)
R29: *Sc 1, inv dec 1,* 6 times. (12 sts)
R30: Inv dec around 6 times. (6 sts)

Fasten off and close piece.

LEAFY TOP

Using green yarn,

Round 1: 6 sc in magic ring (6 sts)
R2: 2 sc in each st around. (12 sts)
R3: *Sc 1, 2 sc in next st,* 6 times. (18 sts)
R4: *Sc 2, 2 sc in next st,* 6 times. (24 sts)
R5: *Sc 1, ch 6 then in 2nd ch from hook- hdc, dc, tr, tr, dc, sk 2 sts and sl st in next st, sc 1,* 5 times (5 total leaves, *photos 1-11*).

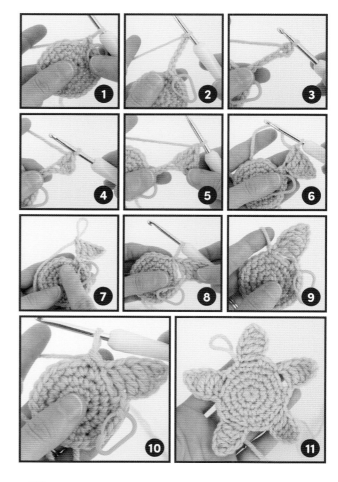

Fasten off and leave an extra long tail for sewing.

Cut a length of green yarn and with a yarn needle, begin to stitch the open gap between R4 and R5 closed *(photos 12-14)*. Weave yarn through the stitches on the back in order to reach the next leaf *(photo 15)*. Secure with a knot and trim tail *(photo 16)*.

 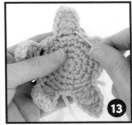   

STEM

Using green yarn,

Round 1: 5 sc in magic ring (5 sts)
R2-5: Sc 5.

Fasten off and leave a tail for sewing.

ASSEMBLY

1. Position the leafy piece to the top of the eggplant *(photos 1 & 2)*. Straight pins come in handy for this part. With the yarn needle, sew around the entire edge of the leafy piece *(photos 3-5)*. Secure with a knot and hide yarn inside the eggplant.

2. Position the stem to the magic ring on the leafy piece. Sew in place and secure with a knot *(photos 6-8)*.

ONION

FINISHED MEASUREMENTS

✕ Approx. 3.5 inches tall by 3.5 inches wide

MATERIALS

✕ Worsted weight yarn: tan and white
✕ Size G/4.25mm crochet hook
✕ Pair of 9mm safety eyes
✕ Black embroidery floss and small embroidery needle
✕ Polyester fiberfill stuffing
✕ Yarn needle
✕ Scissors
✕ Stitch marker
✕ Straight pins (optional, but very helpful when assembling the top piece)

ABBREVIATIONS

✕ Mr – Magic ring
✕ R – Round
✕ Sc – Single crochet
✕ Sts – Stitches
✕ Inv Dec – Invisible decrease
✕ Ch – Chain
✕ Sl St – Slip stitch
✕ Hdc – Half double crochet
✕ Dc – Double crochet

PATTERN NOTES

✕ This pattern is crocheted in continuous rounds

ONION

Using tan yarn,

Round 1: 6 sc in magic ring (6 sts)
R2: 2 sc in each st around. (12 sts)
R3: *Sc 1, 2 sc in next st,* 6 times. (18 sts)
R4: *Sc 2, 2 sc in next st,* 6 times. (24 sts)
R5: *Sc 3, 2 sc in next st,* 6 times. (30 sts)
R6: *Sc 4, 2 sc in next st,* 6 times. (36 sts)
R7: *Sc 5, 2 sc in next st,* 6 times. (42 sts)
R8–15: Sc 42.

Add safety eyes and stitch mouth.

R16: *Sc 5, inv dec 1,* 6 times. (36 sts)
R17: *Sc 4, inv dec 1,* 6 times. (30 sts)
R18: Sc 30.

Begin stuffing with fiberfill and continue as you go.

R19: *Sc 3, inv dec 1,* 6 times. (24 sts)
R20: *Sc 2, inv dec 1,* 6 times. (18 sts)
R21: *Sc 1, inv dec 1,* 6 times. (12 sts)
R22: Inv dec around 6 times. (6 sts)

Fasten off and close piece.

TO ADD THE WHITE ROOT PIECES:

1. Cut about 8 strands of white yarn *(photo 2)*. With one strand, tie a knot on one end and insert the yarn needle on the other. Push the needle through one of the stitches near the bottom of the onion and pull through around R22 *(photos 3–5)*. Repeat for the remaining strands *(photo 6)*. Trim to desired length *(photo 7)*.

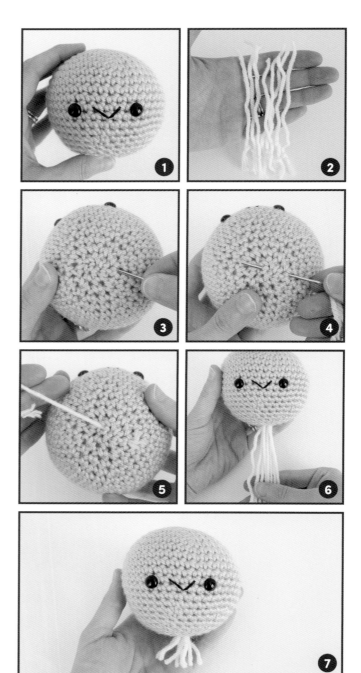

ONION TOP

Using tan yarn,

Ch 12, then sl st into the 1st ch to form a circle. Ch 1, *(photos 1-4)*

Row 1: *Dc and hdc into next stitch, sl st,*, 6 times. *(photos 5 & 6)*

Fasten off and leave a tail for sewing.

Position onion top around the magic ring on the top of the onion *(photos 9 & 10)*. With a yarn needle, sew into place *(photo 11)*. Secure with a knot and hide yarn inside the onion.

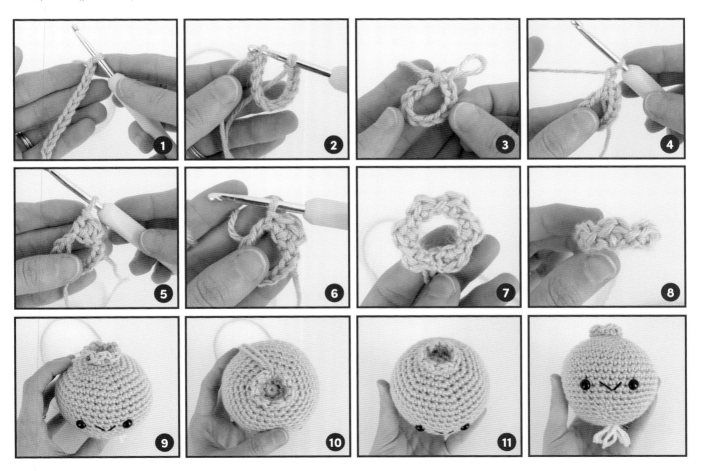

PEACH

FINISHED MEASUREMENTS
- ✕ Approx. 3.5 inches tall by 3 inches wide

MATERIALS
- ✕ Worsted weight yarn: peach, brown, and green
- ✕ Size G/4.25mm crochet hook
- ✕ Pair of 9mm safety eyes
- ✕ Black embroidery floss and small embroidery needle
- ✕ Polyester fiberfill stuffing
- ✕ Yarn needle
- ✕ Scissors
- ✕ Stitch marker
- ✕ Optional:
  - Cheeks – pink felt or pink embroidery floss and size E crochet hook

ABBREVIATIONS
- ✕ Mr – Magic ring
- ✕ R – Round
- ✕ Sc – Single crochet
- ✕ Sts – Stitches
- ✕ Inv Dec – Invisible decrease
- ✕ Ch – Chain
- ✕ Hdc – Half double crochet
- ✕ Dc – Double crochet
- ✕ Tr – Triple crochet

PATTERN NOTES
- ✕ This pattern is crocheted in continuous rounds

PEACH

Using peach yarn,

Round 1: 6 sc in magic ring (6 sts)
R2: 2 sc in each st around. (12 sts)
R3: *Sc 1, 2 sc in next st,* 6 times. (18 sts)
R4: *Sc 2, 2 sc in next st,* 6 times. (24 sts)
R5: *Sc 3, 2 sc in next st,* 6 times. (30 sts)
R6: *Sc 4, 2 sc in next st,* 6 times. (36 sts)
R7: *Sc 5, 2 sc in next st,* 6 times. (42 sts)
R8-13: Sc 42.

Add safety eyes and stitch mouth.

R14: *Sc 5, inv dec 1,* 6 times. (36 sts)
R15: *Sc 4, inv dec 1,* 6 times. (30 sts)
R16: *Sc 3, inv dec 1,* 6 times. (24 sts)

Begin adding fiberfill and continue as you go.

R17: Sc 24.
R18: *Sc 2, inv dec 1,* 6 times. (18 sts)
R19: *Sc 1, inv dec 1,* 6 times. (12 sts)
R20: Inv dec around 6 times. (6 sts)

Fasten off and close piece, leaving a long tail for making indent.

TO MAKE THE INDENT:

1. With the long tail and a yarn needle, insert needle in the middle of R20 *(photo 2)*. Weave needle up through to the middle of the top magic ring (R1, *photo 3*). Pull gently.

2. Bring yarn down on one side of the peach *(photo 4)* and insert needle back into the middle of R20 *(photo 5)*.

3. Weave needle up to the top magic ring (R1) again *(photo 6)*.

4. Bring yarn down on the same side again and insert needle into the middle of R20 *(photo 7)*.

5. The tail will end at the top of the peach *(photo 8)*. Tie a knot and trim tail, hide yarn inside peach.

OPTIONAL:

Felt cheeks – cut two small circles of pink felt and sew near safety eyes.

OR

Crochet cheeks – with pink embroidery floss and Size E hook,

Round 1: 7 sc in magic ring.

Fasten off. Sew near safety eyes.

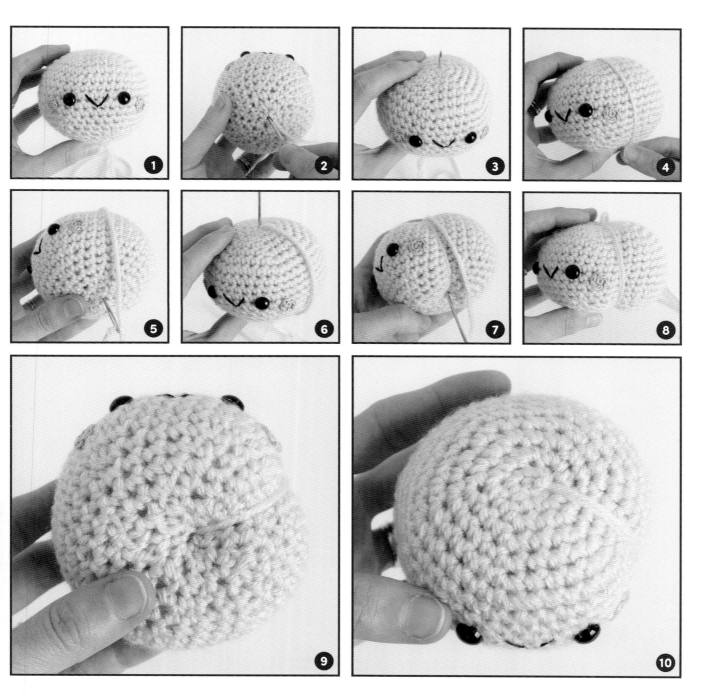

STEM

Using brown yarn,

Round 1: 5 sc in magic ring (5 sts)
R2-6: Sc 5.

Fasten off and leave a tail for sewing.

Position the stem onto the magic ring of the peach. With a yarn needle, sew stem into place.

LEAF: MAKE 1

Using green yarn, Ch 9.

Row 1: Starting in 2nd ch from hook sc, hdc, dc, tr, tr, dc, hdc, sc. (8 sts)

Note: comma represents the next chain.
For example: sc in 2nd ch from hook, hdc in next ch, and so forth until you reach the end of the chain *(photos 1-5)*.

Fasten off and leave a tail for sewing. Attach near the stem *(photo 6)*.

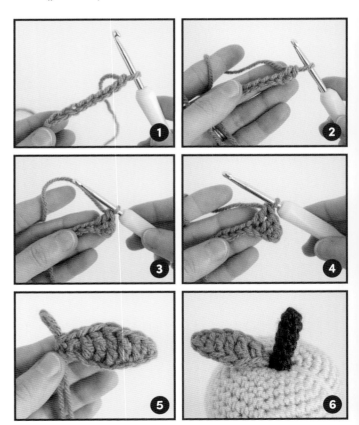

PINEAPPLE

FINISHED MEASUREMENTS
- ✕ Approx. 8.5 inches tall by 4 inches wide

MATERIALS
- ✕ Worsted weight yarn: golden yellow and green
- ✕ Size G/4.25mm crochet hook
- ✕ Pair of 9mm safety eyes
- ✕ Black embroidery floss and small embroidery needle
- ✕ Polyester fiberfill stuffing
- ✕ Yarn needle
- ✕ Scissors
- ✕ Stitch marker
- ✕ Straight pins (optional, but very helpful when assembling the top piece)
- ✕ Optional: a small fabric pouch with plastic pellets (see notes)

ABBREVIATIONS
- ✕ Mr – Magic ring
- ✕ R – Round
- ✕ Sc – Single crochet
- ✕ Sts – Stitches
- ✕ Inv Dec – Invisible decrease

PATTERN NOTES
- ✕ This pattern is crocheted in continuous rounds
- ✕ Pineapple is worked from the bottom to the top. Make sure to place safety eyes and stitch mouth accordingly.
- ✕ To make the pineapple have a sturdy base, add a fabric pouch filled with plastic pellets to the bottom of the pineapple before adding fiberfill. Plastic pellets can be found in craft stores near the fiberfill.

PINEAPPLE BODY

Using golden yellow yarn,

Round 1: 6 sc in magic ring (6 sts)
R2: 2 sc in each st around. (12 sts)
R3: *Sc 1, 2 sc in next st,* 6 times. (18 sts)
R4: *Sc 2, 2 sc in next st,* 6 times. (24 sts)
R5: *Sc 3, 2 sc in next st,* 6 times. (30 sts)
R6: *Sc 4, 2 sc in next st,* 6 times. (36 sts)
R7: *Sc 5, 2 sc in next st,* 6 times. (42 sts)
R8: *Sc 6, 2 sc in next st,* 6 times. (48 sts)
R9–24: Sc 48.

Add safety eyes and stitch mouth *(photo 1)*.

R25: *Sc 6, inv dec 1,* 6 times. (42 sts)
R26: *Sc 5, inv dec 1,* 6 times. (36 sts)
R27: *Sc 4, inv dec 1,* 6 times. (30 sts)

If adding fabric pouch with plastic pellets, do so now *(photo 2)*.

Begin adding fiberfill and continue as you go *(photo 3)*.

R28: *Sc 3, inv dec 1,* 6 times. (24 sts)
R29: *Sc 2, inv dec 1,* 6 times. (18 sts)
R30: *Sc 1, inv dec 1,* 6 times. (12 sts)
R31: Inv dec around 6 times. (6 sts)

Fasten off and close piece.

PINEAPPLE TOP

MEDIUM LEAF: MAKE 4
Using green yarn,

Round 1: 6 sc in magic ring (6 sts)
R2: Sc 6.
R3: 2 sc in each st around. (12 sts)
R4-13: Sc 12.
R14: *Sc 1, inv dec 1,* 4 times. (8 sts)

Fasten off and leave a tail for sewing.

Add fiberfill.

LARGE LEAF: MAKE 4
Using green yarn,

Round 1: 6 sc in magic ring (6 sts)
R2: Sc 6.
R3: 2 sc in each st around. (12 sts)
R4-16: Sc 12.
R17: *Sc 1, inv dec 1,* 4 times. (8 sts)

Fasten off and leave a tail for sewing.

Add fiberfill.

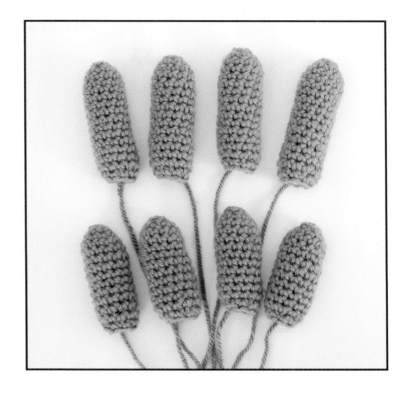

LEAF ASSEMBLY

1. Place 1 large leaf and 2 medium leaves on the top of the pineapple. With a yarn needle, sew into place *(photos 1 & 2)*.

2. For the middle row, place 1 large leaf and 2 medium leaves behind the leaves from step 1 and sew in place *(photos 3 & 4)*.

3. Sew the remaining 2 large leaves behind the leaves from step 2 *(photos 5-7)*.

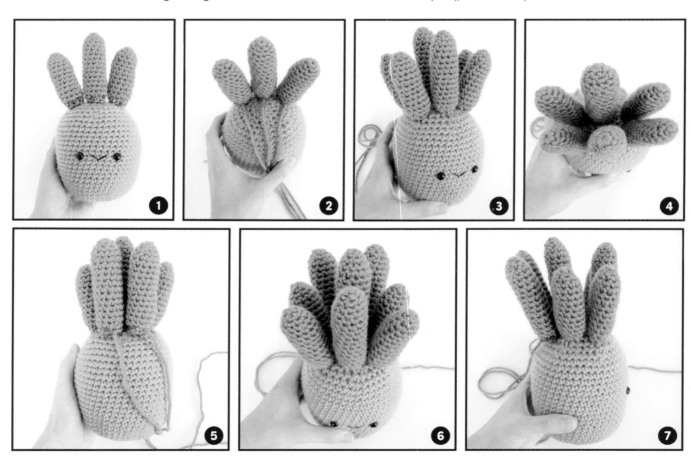

TOMATO

FINISHED MEASUREMENTS
- ✕ Approx. 3 inches tall by 3.5 inches wide

MATERIALS
- ✕ Worsted weight yarn: red and green
- ✕ Size G/4.25mm crochet hook
- ✕ Pair of 9mm safety eyes
- ✕ Black embroidery floss and small embroidery needle
- ✕ Polyester fiberfill stuffing
- ✕ Yarn needle
- ✕ Scissors
- ✕ Stitch marker
- ✕ Straight pins (optional, but very helpful when assembling the top piece)

ABBREVIATIONS
- ✕ Mr – Magic ring
- ✕ R – Round
- ✕ Sc – Single crochet
- ✕ Sts – Stitches
- ✕ Inv Dec – Invisible decrease
- ✕ Ch – Chain
- ✕ Sl St – Slip stitch

PATTERN NOTES
- ✕ This pattern is crocheted in continuous rounds

TOMATO

Using red yarn,

Round 1: 6 sc in magic ring (6 sts)
R2: 2 sc in each st around. (12 sts)
R3: *Sc 1, 2 sc in next st,* 6 times. (18 sts)
R4: *Sc 2, 2 sc in next st,* 6 times. (24 sts)
R5: *Sc 3, 2 sc in next st,* 6 times. (30 sts)
R6: *Sc 4, 2 sc in next st,* 6 times. (36 sts)
R7: *Sc 5, 2 sc in next st,* 6 times. (42 sts)
R8: *Sc 6, 2 sc in next st,* 6 times. (48 sts)
R9–16: Sc 48.

Add safety eyes and stitch mouth.

R17: *Sc 6, inv dec 1,* 6 times. (42 sts)
R18: *Sc 5, inv dec 1,* 6 times. (36 sts)
R19: *Sc 4, inv dec 1,* 6 times. (30 sts)
R20: *Sc 3, inv dec 1,* 6 times. (24 sts)

Begin stuffing with fiberfill and continue as you go.

R21: *Sc 2, inv dec 1,* 6 times. (18 sts)
R22: *Sc 1, inv dec 1,* 6 times. (12 sts)
R23: Inv dec around 6 times. (6 sts)

Fasten off and close piece.

LEAF

Using green yarn,

Round 1: 6 sc in magic ring (6 sts)
R2: 2 sc in each st around. (12 sts)
R3: *Sc 1, ch 3 then in 2nd ch from hook sc 1 in each ch across (2 sc total), sl st into original sc, sc 1 into the next st,* 6 times. (6 leaves total, *photos 1-7*)

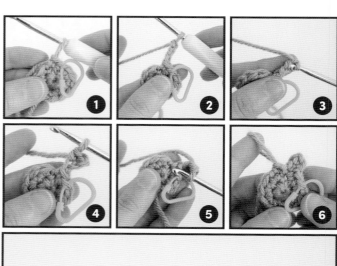

Fasten off and leave a tail for sewing.

Position piece on top of tomato *(photo 8)*. Insert the needle into both the leaf and tomato, bringing the needle back up to the leaf piece *(photos 9 & 10)*. With a yarn needle, weave it between **R2** and **R3** *(photo 11)*. The stitching will form a horizontal line of stitches between **R2** and **R3** *(photos 12 & 13)*.

Secure with a knot and hide yarn inside the tomato.

Lauren Espy's journey with crochet began in 2009 when her grandmother gifted her a book about amigurumi, the Japanese art of knitting or crocheting small, stuffed creatures. In 2015, Lauren opened her Etsy shop, A Menagerie of Stitches. While Lauren was working at a nature and science museum, she became inspired to crochet a chemistry set, complete with beakers, test tubes, and a Bunsen burner. What started as a hobby quickly developed into a passion and then a career. She shares her designs with an ever-growing Instagram audience @amenagerieofstitches.

When not crocheting, Lauren loves to go on road trips and spend time with her husband, Carl.